INSIGHT

EXPLORE
SAN FRANCISCO

D0192168

CONTENTS

Introduction

Directory

Credits

Best Routes

ARCHITECTURE BUFFS

Admire grand hotels on Nob Hill (route 7), the Beaux Arts buildings in Civic Center (route 6), modern museums in South of Market (route 5), and charming Victorians in the Haight and Castro (routes 9 and 10).

RECOMMENDED ROUTES FOR...

ART ENTHUSIASTS

Head to South of Market for modern and cartoon art (route 5), Civic Center for the Asian Art Museum (route 6), Golden Gate Park for the de Young Museum (route 9), or the Mission for colorful murals (route 11).

CHILDREN

Enjoy barking sea lions, an aquarium, and antique arcade games at Fisherman's Wharf (route 1), explore the Children's Creativity Museum (route 5) or ride the vintage merry-go-round in Golden Gate Park (route 9).

CHURCHES AND TEMPLES

See the old Mission Dolores that gave the Mission District its name (route 11), tiny temples in Chinatown (route 4), the Gothic Grace Cathedral on Nob Hill (route 7), and Saints Peter and Paul Church in North Beach (route 3).

FOODIES

Visit North Beach for Italian food (route 3), the Mission for burritos (route 11), Fisherman's Wharf for fresh seafood (route 1), and the central neighborhoods for chic eateries (routes 7 and 8).

LITERARY TYPES

Pay homage to Beat writers in North Beach (route 3), rifle through anarchist literature in the Haight (route 9), and visit the inspiration for Armistead Maupin's Barbary Lane on Russian Hill (route 7).

PARKS AND GARDENS

Enjoy Golden Gate Park's lakes and botanical gardens (route 9); hang with hipsters at the Mission's Dolores Park (route 11); relax by a lagoon at the Palace of Fine Arts (route 12); or picnic at a Pacific Heights park (route 8).

SHOPPERS

Peruse Union Square's emporia (route 5), Jackson Square's antiques (route 3), Hayes Street's boutiques (route 6), home decor and clothing on Fillmore and Union streets (route 8), and thrift stores in the Haight (route 9).

INTRODUCTION

An introduction to San Francisco's geography, customs and culture, plus illuminating background information on cuisine, history and what to do when you're there.

Golden Gate Bridge

EXPLORE SAN FRANCISCO

Built on sloping hills next to sparkling waters, San Francisco is often called the most beautiful American city. Many visitors are attracted by the city's open-minded character, fertile ground for idealists and entrepreneurial gold-prospectors alike.

With dramatic views from impossibly steep hills, inventive cuisine that caters to foodies, diverse cultural attractions, and vibrant neighborhoods, San Francisco is an easy city to love. Often considered the most European of large American cities, the lively, compact metropolis spans some 49 square miles (127 sq km), broken up by 43 windswept and fog-capped hills. These scattered slopes define the city's skyline and urban landscape, offering arresting views of elegant bridges and the glistening blue-green Pacific and San Francisco Bay.

Hidden gems

Tucked on and around the hills of San Francisco are dozens of small, distinct neighborhoods with their own microclimates, stereotypes, and special attractions. Landmarks like Alcatraz, the Golden Gate Bridge, Chinatown, and the city's cable-cars, as well as the endless array of lesser known attractions – mural-lined alleys, a literary festival, and a 1910 hardware store that sells just about everything! – all contribute to the special charm of the City by the Bay.

CITY DEVELOPMENT

San Francisco is no stranger to the spotlight on the world's stage. Throughout the city's history, more than one boom and bust has drawn international attention. In the 19th century, the discovery of gold in the Sierra foothills ignited the largest mass migration in history, with treasure-seekers flooding the then small town of 2,000 and turning it into a proper city of 10 times that size. In 1906, the world's attention was drawn to San Francisco when it was struck by a massive earthquake measuring an estimated 8.3 on the Richter scale. Coupled with the ensuing fire that raged for three days, the earthquake left the city in ruins. Then, later in the 20th century, the San Francisco Bay Area witnessed first-hand the prosperous dot-com era and its subsequent rapid unraveling.

Center stage

The city has also attracted attention for its significant role in political moments and countercultural movements. The stage of the War Memorial Opera House saw the signing of the United

Beat Museum mural   *Capturing the San Francisco scene*

Nations permanent charter in 1945. Then, in the late 1950s, North Beach became Beat-central, attracting writers such as Jack Kerouac, Allen Ginsberg, Lawrence Ferlinghetti, Philip Whalen, and Michael McClure.

In 1967, thousands of hippies descended on Haight-Ashbury and Golden Gate Park during the "Summer of Love." More recently, the city has become a focal point for the gay community's battles for equal rights; when Mayor Gavin Newsome began signing same-sex marriage licenses in 2004, the gay marriage issue became a national talking point.

Contemporary appeal

Yet, no matter what dramas befall this city, its charms only seem to grow. Millions of visitors come each year to absorb San Francisco's legacy, explore Alcatraz, admire stunning views, dine on first-class cuisine, shop to their hearts' content, and climb impossibly steep hills in the city's iconic cable-cars. Whichever aspect of San Francisco intrigues, most visitors find it is difficult not to leave one's heart here.

GEOGRAPHY

At just 7 sq miles (18 sq km) and with a population of around 800,000, San Francisco is small for a major city in terms of both geography and population. Yet, for a city of such narrow limits, San Francisco covers a huge spectrum of natural and social terrain.

The city sits on a bay over 400 sq miles (1,000 sq km) in area, which is crossed by five bridges. One of these bridges is the world-famous Golden Gate Bridge, which was completed in 1937 and still remains an enduring, defining symbol of San Francisco. Space in the compact city is at a premium today, with real-estate prices among the highest in the country.

Diverse neighborhoods

There is a very strong sense of neighborhood in San Francisco, with locals taking immense pride in their home and promoting a stronger sense of community than is found in many other cities of similar stature. There are over a dozen neighborhood enclaves, each

Don't Call It Frisco

The surest way of giving yourself away as a tourist in San Francisco is to call the city "Frisco." Newspaperman Herb Caen, chronicler of things San Franciscan, felt strongly enough to name his book *Don't Call It Frisco*. Unpopular with locals since the 1930s, the name is not a corruption of Francisco, but is thought to be from an old English word, *frithsoken*, meaning refuge, and was used by sailors to refer to a port with repair yards. Another nickname to avoid? *San Fran*. Instead, blend in with the locals by calling it "SF" or simply, "The City."

San Francisco skyline

with a distinct culture and identity, including the bustling Chinatown, multicultural North Beach, gritty Tenderloin, Latino- and hipster-dominated Mission, gay-friendly Castro, alternative Haight-Ashbury, upper-crust Pacific Heights, tony Russian Hill, old-fashioned Nob Hill, and preppy, post-collegiate Marina and Cow Hollow.

San Francisco's outlying districts are equally distinctive. For instance, the vast, residential Sunset and Richmond districts are home to many Russian, Irish, and Chinese families, and offer commercial hubs filled with bookstores, grocery stores, and Asian restaurants. The Richmond is also bisected by Lincoln Park, home to the Palace of the Legion of Honor, wild coastline trails, and lucky views of the Golden Gate Bridge.

CLIMATE

The city's climate is generally agreeable, but can vary from hour to hour and even between neighborhoods. Spring is warm and sunny, while summer is cooler and overcast, with the city often blanketed in fog. Come the fall, the city's real summer swings into effect, with mild and sunny days. The majority of the rainfall occurs in December and January, though crisp, sunny days offer respite from those that are damp and cloudy.

Contrary to the common misconception of a lush California, much of the state is, in fact, a semi-desert. Its Mediterranean climate, where 98 percent of its annual rainfall occurs between November and March, leaves it vulnerable to drought and wildfires the rest of the year. Still, these natural hazards, along with the possibility of earthquakes and the reality of frequent fog, do little to quell the city's popularity.

Earthquakes

From its plunging cliffs to its dramatic peaks and valley, the astounding natural beauty of the Bay Area is the result of shifting tectonic plates. Sitting between two major seismic fault lines – the San Andreas skirting the edge of the city and the Hayward running up the East Bay – San Francisco is continually under threat of jolts that can cause millions of dollars' worth of damage. Fortunately, improved building codes and "retrofitting" (structural revamping) have stabilized all the bridges, highway overpasses, and downtown buildings that suffered in previous quakes.

Despite the threat, San Franciscans handle the subject of earthquakes with great aplomb, shrugging their shoulders with a "What can you do?" attitude. Still, every California school kid learns the basic rules: if an earthquake occurs, stay indoors, preferably under something sturdy like a piece of furniture or in a doorframe; if outside, avoid trees, power lines, buildings, and bridges.

Eye-catching auto repair shop sign

SF resident

THE PEOPLE

San Francisco is truly a multicultural city, with diverse demographics representing all ethnicities and proclivities. The Chinatown area is famous, but San Francisco also has a vibrant Hispanic-origin population and large communities of people of Italian, Japanese, Russian, and Southeast Asian descent. Indeed, only 35 percent of San Franciscans were born in California, while 39 percent were born outside of the U.S. San Francisco is known internationally for its large gay and lesbian population, which crosses all

DON'T LEAVE SAN FRANCISCO WITHOUT...

Sampling the Ferry Building farmers market. There's no better way to spend a Saturday morning than tasting your way through the fresh fruit, local cheese, salumi, flavored olive oils, and other artisanal offerings here. See page 15.

Book-browsing at the City Lights Bookstore. Pay homage to the city's literary tradition at this Beat landmark owned by Lawrence Ferlinghetti. See page 37.

Riding a cable car. As the 1910 landmarks rumble and ding over Nob Hill at a deliberate 9.5 mph, it's impossible not to enjoy yourself. Take the scenic Powell-Hyde route for a peek down crooked Lombard Street. See page 32.

Exploring a Secret Garden-esque staircase. With serene atmosphere and gorgeous views, the garden-lined staircases of Telegraph Hill and Russian Hill are some of the prettiest and most quietly intriguing blocks in the city. See page 39 and 61.

A night at the museum. Every Thursday evening, the California Academy of Sciences transforms into a popular (and kid-free) social event; the Exploratorium does the same every first Thursday of the month. See page 72.

Ordering an Irish coffee at the Buena Vista. After all, it was invented here! See page 32.

Experiencing the Mission like a local. Hit up one of the sunny district's famed *taquerías*, then relax at Dolores Park – easily the city's biggest park scene in the city on weekends – or burn off your burrito walking past bold murals and offbeat shops. See page 79.

Playing old-fashioned penny arcade games. Musée Méchanique is a must-see in Fisherman's Wharf. Bring a pocket-full of quarters! See page 30.

Walking through the heart of Chinatown. Stroll bustling, lantern-lined Grant Street and picturesque Waverly Place, and nibble fresh fortune cookies in Ross Alley. See page 41.

Soaking up views of the bridges – yes, both of them. Walk or bike the famous Golden Gate Bridge, or admire it while sipping a martini at the Top of the Mark. The Bay Bridge – with its eye-catching LED lightshow – is just as impressive at night. See page 89.

Picnic in Dolores Park

ethnic divisions and wields significant political power in the city. Many are attracted to San Francisco by its liberal, accommodating spirit. Tolerance is part of the city's ethos, not to mention public policy: tolerance of cultural, religious, racial, and gender divergences are hard-wired into the city's civic codes and legislation.

Living standards

The general standard of living is high, and the average earnings of residents enable enough eating out and nights on the town to sustain the city's dining and cultural establishments. However, San Francisco also has a large and visible homeless population. Initiatives are making a difference, but visitors will undoubtedly notice the many down-and-outs.

HEALTH AND ENVIRONMENT

San Francisco has rightly developed a reputation for being very eco-friendly, with a broad recycling program (even composting is required), a significant bike-riding population, some of the world's toughest anti-pollution laws, and countless campaigns to "green" the city by planting trees and native species on rooftops and in public places. Nevertheless, it is also a densely populated metropolitan area that carries inevitable environmental concerns, ranging from air quality to water shortages.

San Franciscans are also notoriously concerned with the health of their bodies and souls. There is an abundance of gyms and yoga studios, natural food stores and fresh farmers markets, spas and alternative health practitioners, and vegetarian and even vegan restaurants.

Recreation

Having a good time is an easy order to obey in the city that lays claim to the first espresso on the West Coast and to being the home of the Martini. The rich nightlife, food, and cultural pickings ensure that foodies, film buffs, bar-hoppers, jazz fiends, aspiring poets, and 1960s nostalgists all have plenty to enjoy.

The city is home to numerous museums, with the majority clustered downtown and in the South of Market district, although a number are strewn about outlying neighborhoods. The heavy-hitters include the San Francisco Museum of Modern Art (SFMOMA), the Legion of Honor, the de Young, and the Asian Art Museum. Several other museums celebrate San Francisco's history and its ethnically diverse population.

Fresh-air enthusiasts are also spoiled for choice in San Francisco, with nearly every kind of outdoor activity on offer, from sailing and windsurfing on the bay to biking, baseball, basketball, tennis, polo, and fly-fishing in the sprawling Golden Gate Park, the urban oasis that stretches 52 city blocks from the Haight-Ashbury neighborhood to the ocean.

Musée Mécanique   *Powell–Hyde line cable car*

TOP TIPS

Advance booking. Since San Francisco is a very popular convention and tourist town, it's important to make reservations well ahead of time, both for hotels, Alcatraz tours, and any popular restaurants on your must-eat list. An advantage of booking hotels by phone is that you can request a view, which can make or break a hotel room in San Francisco.

Getting around. For frequent travel on buses, it's worth buying a pass; these can be bought to cover one, three, or seven days, or a month. Visit www.sfmta.com for details. To find out when your bus is actually coming (as opposed to the scheduled time) visit www.nextmuni.com for real-time data.

Parking. Parking in San Francisco can be difficult to find and expensive. See www.sfmta.com/getting-around/parking for information on open lots and spaces, what curb and meter colors mean, street sweeping and holiday exceptions, and other general rules.

Open for business. Most shops are open every day, but with shorter hours on Sunday (typical hours are Mon–Sat 10am–7pm and Sun noon–6pm). Many restaurants are closed on Mondays.

Restaurant reservations. Need a dinner reservation for tonight? You can skip the hassle of calling multiple individual restaurants to check availability by using Open Table (www.opentable.com). The popular website allows you to search by multiple criteria – including time, neighborhood, cuisine, party size, and price –

then book your reservation online. For all the latest San Francisco restaurant news, check http://sf.eater.com.

Tipping. Tipping in the U.S. is not optional: 15–18 percent is standard, and 20 percent means you were happy with both service and food. Percentages are calculated pre-tax. A quick way of calculating is to double the tax (8.5 percent) and round up or down depending on level of satisfaction.

Dress codes. Going out in San Francisco isn't necessarily a fancy affair and few restaurants or bars have dress codes. Only the nightclubs and top-notch restaurants truly merit dress-up attire, though in some mid-range restaurants you may feel more comfortable in something a step up from T-shirt and sneakers.

Tickets. Discount tickets can be bought for shows and other events from the TIX kiosk at Union Square.

Getting in. Most bars and clubs are 21 and over, with I.D. required at the door. At dive bars, cash-only policies are common, but the bartender can usually point you to the nearest ATM (sometimes in the bar itself). Entrance fees are also usually cash only.

First Tuesdays and Thursdays. On the first Tuesday of the month, many museums offer free admission. On the first Thursday of each month, the San Francisco tradition of "First Thursdays" turns typically calm galleries into lively, wine-sipping social events. Many galleries schedule their show openings and then keep their doors open later than usual.

Restaurants on Columbus Avenue

FOOD AND DRINK

California wine and cuisine, cultural diversity, celebrity chefs, and bounty from the sea and land – the City by the Bay is a foodie's delight, with something for all culinary persuasions.

Nothing has changed since the writer Alice B. Toklas referred in 1954 to her San Francisco dining experiences with her partner Gertrude Stein as "gastronomic orgies." The city continues to delight food-and-drink lovers, and has emerged as one of the culinary capitals of the world. Blessed with year-round natural abundance, thriving immigrant communities, and a slight spirit of rebellion, San Francisco appeals to all tastes. Authentic ethnic eateries serve dishes from cultures all over the globe, and the hugely popular California cuisine promotes the use of locally grown, in-season ingredients. From fresh breads and delicate pastries at cafés to delectable small plates at esteemed fine-dining establishments courtesy of celebrity chefs, the extensive menu of enticements is virtually impossible to abstain from in this "Paris of the West."

INTERNATIONAL FLAVORS

San Francisco's international gastronomic influences began early on. From the mid-19th century, immigrants contributed considerable diversity to the city's culinary character: adding to the Mexican and American traditions already present, Chinese, French, Irish, German, Basque, Spanish, and Italian immigrants brought with them the tastes of home – dishes such as *Cioppino*, a fish stew that Italian fishermen brought with them from Genoa and adapted by using the sea's bounty from San Francisco Bay, typically dungeness crab, clams, shrimp, scallops, squid, mussels, and fish with fresh tomatoes in a wine sauce.

To this day, immigrants continue to introduce dishes that broaden the city's palate, as evidenced by the city's Ethiopian, Arabian, Moroccan, Afghan, and Turkish restaurants. Thanks to San Francisco's position on the edge of the Pacific Ocean, its pan-Asian and Pacific Rim cuisine remains especially strong and diverse.

SUSTAINABLE FOOD MOVEMENT

The Bay Area is very well known for its attention to health and the environment. It is unsurprising, then, that celebrity chefs and food artisans have in recent years managed to turn the region into the epicenter of the Amer-

Haute cuisine

ican sustainable food movement. This is based on the belief that food should be produced locally and using techniques based on age-old traditions. Chef Alice Waters is credited with starting this culinary revolution; in 1971 she gave birth to "California cuisine," when she opened the now-famous Chez Panisse restaurant in Berkeley. "California cuisine" is typified by seasonal, usually organic, local produce. Flavor combinations accentuate freshness, subtlety, and texture, and meat is not always the focal point. The cuisine highlights the Bay Area's natural cornucopia, and its wild popularity has resulted in an impressive assortment of boutique charcuteries, cheese makers, bakeries, and superb farmers' markets. One of the best places to see the local passion for food is at the Ferry Building. Once a thriving terminal, the long and graceful building with its distinctive clock tower is now an airy marketplace flush with specialty food purveyors including Cow Girl Creamery, Hog Island Oyster Company, Prather Ranch Meat Co., Acme Bread, and McEvoy Ranch Olive Oil.

PLACES TO EAT

Cafés

San Francisco loves its café culture: the importance to locals of Italian-style, espresso-based coffee, mouth-watering light meals, and ready Wi-Fi access should not be underestimated. Coffee has evolved into an art form here, with roasters like Blue Bottle Coffee and Ritual Coffee Roasters approaching coffee brewing with as much passion as wine makers approach wine. In addition to excellent coffee and teas, most cafés also offer a menu of sandwiches, salads, soups, bagels, breakfast muffins, and pastries. Specialty teas are also popular,

Daily bread

Bread has long been a San Francisco specialty. With yeast in short supply, settlers who arrived in the Gold Rush utilized fermented dough as the basis of their bread. This technique hardly originated with this generation of gold-seekers, but San Francisco is home to natural yeasts and air-borne bacteria that create the chewy texture and sour taste that define San Franciscan sourdough. In addition to sourdough from Boudin at the Wharf (see page 32), locals get their daily bread from many local bakeries. North Beach's Liguria Bakery (see page 40) is a go-to for fresh-from-the-oven focaccia, and Stella Pastry and Café Bakery (446 Columbus Avenue at Green) is beloved for its *sacripantina*. La Boulange (see page 113) has 13 outposts in the city serving fresh organic breads and French pastries, and Tartine Bakery (see page 83) is a Mission must for decadent tarts.

Joe's Crab Shack

and are found in cafés as well as tea-houses. Downtown, especially in the Financial District, major coffee chains are ubiquitous, but in other neighbor-hoods local independent coffee roast-ers and cafés thrive, Even at 11am on a Wednesday, cafés are crowded with local laptop-toting freelance workers; their fondness for camping out for hours at a time can sometimes make finding space a challenge.

Neighborhood bars and eateries

Neighborhood restaurants run the gamut from hole-in-the-wall Thai or sushi spots to trendy white-tablecloth affairs, and from friendly French bis-tros to even friendlier German beer halls. Small-plate restaurants are pop-ular, and many bars also have a kitchen serving either pub fare or more upscale snacks and small plates, depending on the establishment.

High-end restaurants

From French to fusion, the menus at San Francisco's hottest tables are first-class, and you will need to reserve, often far in advance. The highest concentration of fine dining is found downtown, from the Financial District to the Embarcadero and South of Market. However, many top-notch restaurants are on the backstreets or scattered in far-flung neighbor-hoods. For excellent, up-to-the-minute advice, the concierge of a fancy hotel is always a good bet, or check out www.yelp.com, http://sfeater.com, as well as www.opentable.com.

WHAT TO EAT

Around the city, many neighborhoods are known for a particular cuisine. The Mission's many *taquerías* offer raved-about burritos, North Beach serves Ital-ian and excellent espresso, Polk Street has a high concentration of small Thai restaurants, the Tenderloin is known for Indian and Vietnamese food, and while Chinatown is an easy choice for Chi-nese, the Richmond District's Clement Street is also filled with authentic fare that is sometimes harder to find among Chinatown's tourist traps. Fisherman's Wharf is always crowded with sea-food-lovers, but mid-November through May is particularly busy, with locals enticed by Dungeness crabs steamed, cracked, drowned in butter, and accom-panied by San Francisco's famous sour-dough bread. Throughout the city, plenty of attention is paid to vegetarians and even vegans, even in restaurants that also serve meat.

EATING PATTERNS

On weekdays, breakfast is generally between 7am and 10am. In all corners of the city, people line up for morning lattes to bring to work. On weekends, lines wrap around corners all morning for leisurely brunches, with service run-ning into the early afternoon. Brunch

Smart vegetarian dish

A welcoming cocktail

can be a hearty affair, from omelets with fresh veggies and cheeses to pancakes with fruit. Those with a lighter appetite nibble on pastries and bagels at cafés, and are not shy about lingering hours to read the newspaper and catch up with friends. Weekday lunch is between 11.30am and 2.30pm and dinner starts around 5.30pm, although locals rarely venture out to dinner before 7pm and few restaurants seat past 10pm.

DRINKING CULTURE

San Franciscans love their libations. Surrounded by wine country, the city is a convenient gateway for visiting the many acclaimed vineyards in its vicinity and trying an excellent selection of local wine, from traditional varietals such as Chardonnay and Cabernet, to lesser-known specialties such as Gamay Beaujolais. The proximity to wine country also means San Francisco is filled with well-informed wine critics, and those aspiring to be so. Wine bars are increasingly popular, especially in the central neighborhoods and downtown.

If beer is your beverage, there are many drinking establishments in San Francisco where it is the clear focus. As well as Belgian beer bars and Guinness-pouring Irish pubs, the city has several large, industrial brewpubs. Residents began brewing their own beer early on in the city's history, and nowadays there are microbreweries producing beers with the strength and complexity to rival any cocktail or glass of wine. One of the standouts is the Anchor Steam Brewery, which not only makes beer, but gin and rye bourbon as well.

Cocktails are no humdrum affair either, with "mixologists" behind the bars at destinations such as the Alembic, Bourbon and Branch, and Rye turning out Sazeracs, Pisco Sours, cucumber and basil gimlets, and other exceptionally creative and tasty concoctions.

Chocolate heaven

Whether you crave Belgian buttercreams or Swiss champagne truffles, San Francisco can come to your rescue. Choose from more than 150 kinds of premium chocolate bars from around the world at Fog City News (www.fogcitynews.com), feast on a giant sundae in Ghirardelli Square (see page 32), or sip a deliciously rich hot chocolate drink at Blue Bottle Coffee Company (see page 57). Local artisan chocolate boutiques are also perfect for finding one-of-a-kind indulgences or lavish gifts. Recchiuti (www.recchiutti.com) offers exquisite confections featuring drawings from local artists and CocoaBella Chocolates (www.cocoabella.com) offers beautifully decorated truffles in exotic flavors such as rosemary caramel, pina colada, and lime chachaca.

Ghirardelli's Chocolate Shop

SHOPPING

Something for everyone is found downtown among the modern shopping centers, affordable retail outposts, and international luxury designers, while boutiques in other neighborhoods cater to distinctive kinds of shopping wish lists.

When the shopping urge strikes, San Francisco is an excellent city to be in. The cosmopolitan spread of merchandise includes gourmet foods, antiques and artwork, whimsical home decor, designer fashions, secondhand thrift, music, and offbeat gifts galore.

fairs that are held throughout the year such as Urban Air Market (www.urba-nairmarket.com), where local designers showcase and sell their wares. San Francisco Fashion Week (www.fashion-week-sf.com), launched in 2004, continues to gain steam.

LOCAL DESIGN

As the birthplace of blue jeans and behemoth Gap Inc., it is no surprise that San Francisco's fashion sense is dominated by denim and other casuals. Still, the common ultra-relaxed look is joined by others that up the fashion ante. Hipster haunts in the Mission and Haight neighborhoods are swarmed by frightfully cool twenty- and thirtysome-things in edgy, attitude-laced outfits, while the smart central neighborhoods are strolled by carefully coifed urban sophisticates in preppy and Euro-chic designer outfits.

San Francisco has a strong independent design culture, evidenced not only by the locally made clothing, jewelry, accessories, housewares, and crafts carried by boutiques, but also by the large turnout at design and shopping

WHERE TO SHOP

Downtown

San Francisco's shopping pulse thumps most wildly in the Union Square neighborhood. Streets are stacked with elegant emporia (Saks Fifth Avenue, Neiman Marcus, Barney's New York, and Nordstrom and Bloomingdales inside the Westfield Centre) and glossy boutiques for international designers such as Cartier, Chanel, Coach, Gucci, Hermès, Louis Vuitton, Prada, Thomas Pink, and Wilkes Bashford. Also here are major American retail outposts (the GAP, Williams-Sonoma, Anthropologie, Urban Outfitters, H&M, Forever 21) and San Francisco institutions such as Gumps, Scheuer Linens, and Britex Fabrics.

For the best selection of antiques, head to historic Jackson Square (www.

Souvenir cable cars   *Window display in Telegraph Hill*

jacksonsquaresf.com), on the southwest corner of the Financial District. On the other side of the Financial District is the Ferry Building, a go-to for gourmands and homebodies, with upscale food purveyors, home and garden shops, and an outstanding farmers' market on Tuesdays, Thursdays, and Saturdays.

Best streets for boutique hopping

Pacific Heights' Fillmore Street (between Post and Pacific) and Presidio Heights' Sacramento Street (between Lyon and Maple) offer a wealth of luxury delicacies, particularly high-end clothing and interior-decor shops. If European shoes, Florentine soaps, and vintage French furnishings are out of your budget, these are still picturesque streets on which to window-shop.

Also devoid of chains, Hayes Street (between Franklin and Laguna) in Hayes Valley is a cheerfully artsy and unique mix of art galleries, cafés, eateries, and boutiques supplying posh footwear, mod travel accessories, handsome home furnishings, upscale body products, and obscure sake.

Sophisticated clusters of jewelry shops, mainstream beauty outlets, clothing boutiques, and chic eateries make Cow Hollow one of the most popular high-end shopping destinations in the city. Try Union Street (between Franklin and Steiner) and Chestnut (from Fillmore Street to Divisadero).

The Mission, meanwhile, offers more varied fare: ethnic threads, Latin jazz CDs, refurbished furniture, fedoras and porkpies, politico literature, unusual housewares, independent designer boutiques, and curiosity shops.

Other neighborhoods

North of Market Street, Chinatown is a bustling bazaar year-round, brimming with tea-selling apothecaries, sidewalk souvenir racks, cramped shops, and fresh-produce stands. Tourists flood Grant Avenue while locals grocery-shop on Stockton Street.

Further north, artsy bookstores, chocolate truffles, Italian bakeries and delicatessens, European lingerie, premium denim, flirty dresses, quaint curios, and antique maps are the order of the day in North Beach.

In posh Russian Hill, Polk Street offers high-end progressive women's fashion, lacy lingerie, vintage and consignment fare; as it heads south for the Tenderloin, low-end clothing and other eclectic stores are more common.

Down in Japantown, the Japan Center (see page 64) supplies everything from vintage silk kimonos to culinary ingredients. Upper Haight offers a scruffy jumble of secondhand, vintage, and contemporary clothing stores, plus trendy shoe shops, independent music stores, and head shops selling all manner of smoking paraphernalia.

In the Castro, expect to find fashionable men's clothing and gay-oriented specialty stores, and the nation's largest gay-and-lesbian-themed bookstore.

Buskers on the pier

ENTERTAINMENT

San Francisco is home to world-class dance, theater, opera, symphony companies, and dozens of clubs. And because of its diminutive size, most forms of entertainment are only a walk or a bus ride away from the city center.

San Franciscans are an adventurous and diverse lot where entertainment is concerned. The city is rich with artistic types and well-informed critics who nurture a vibrant cultural scene that includes both traditional artistic expressions such as opera, symphony, and ballet, and also more avant-garde forms. With its open-minded atmosphere and taste for pushing boundaries, the Bay Area has particularly built a reputation for itself as a breeding ground for experimental and often outrageous work.

MUSIC

Classical and opera

San Francisco has long cherished classical music. In the city's early days, this passion was so great that fire brigades escorted favorite divas through the crowds to performances. San Francisco soon became a regular stop for European troupes, and the tradition still continues: today there are no fewer than seven opera companies in the Bay Area. There are also more classical concerts per capita here than in any other city in the country, a phenomenon described by one critic as an "unreasonable profusion." Chamber music is well served too, with peaceful churches often hosting the small, talented groups.

Jazz

The Lower Fillmore neighborhood was undoubtedly once the city's hopping hotbed of jazz music. During the 1940s it became known as the "Harlem of the West," attracting legends such as Ella Fitzgerald, Duke Ellington, Billie Holiday, Charles Mingus, and Charlie Parker. Today the Fillmore is home to the San Francisco outpost of Yoshi's – a very well-respected Oakland jazz club – but jazz clubs are also found in other parts of the city, particularly downtown.

Contemporary

The city is no stranger to staying on top of current music trends. Light shows held at the Fillmore and Avalon Ballroom became the standard for rock gigs all around the world. In the 1960s locally based artists including Grateful Dead, Jefferson Airplane, and Janis Joplin regularly appeared at these venues, and performed in high-profile concerts in Golden Gate Park. Now, the Bay

Stern Grove Festival

Area's eclectic music scene includes everything from electronica to indie pop, and hip-hop. Large venues include the Warfield Theater, the Fillmore, Great American Music Hall, and Slims; more intimate venues are also popular.

THEATER

San Francisco's early theater tradition started with a proliferation of melodeons (theater-bar-music halls) but more "serious" theater picked up at the turn of the 20th century. In 1967, director Bill Ball led the American Conservatory Theater to its San Francisco premiere, and it soon became a theater with a national reputation. Today, the theater district is centered just west of Union Square on Geary Street. Major commercial theaters stage Broadway hits, while non-profits such as the Magic Theater push new pieces and playwrights, and also premieres early works by major playwrights such as Sam Shepard. Come fall, the San Francisco Fringe Festival serves up untraditional and uncensored fare.

BARS AND CLUBS

San Francisco nightlife options are across the board, from Union Square hotel bars to punk-rock dives, cozy wine bars, intimate comedy venues, and large dance clubs. Live bands and local DJs spin at smaller venues, while more massive clubs draw international DJs. Many of these nightspots are hybrid affairs, blurring the lines between bars, lounges, and clubs. The liveliest neighborhoods after nightfall are the Mission District, the Marina, South of Market, and North Beach.

Festivals

January: Dine About Town; Noir City Film Festival, San Francisco Sketchfest
February: Noise Pop; Lunar New Year Parade; Independent Film Festival; Spike and Mike's Festival of Animation
March: Anarchist Book Fair; St Patrick's Day Parade
April: Perpetual Indulgence in the Park; Cherry Blossom Festival
May: Cinco de Mayo; San Francisco International Film Festival; Bay to Breakers; Carnaval; Mission Creek Music and Arts Festival
June: Silent Film Festival; San Francisco International LGBT Film Festival; North Beach Festival; Haight Street Fair; San Francisco Celebration and Pride Parade; Stern Grove Festival
July: AIDS Walk; San Francisco Shakespeare Festival; San Francisco Jewish Film Festival; Fillmore Jazz Festival
August: Outside Lands
September: Fringe Festival; Free Opera in the Park; Folsom Street Fair; Ghirardelli Square Chocolate Festival
October: Litquake; Castro Street Fair; Hardly Strictly Bluegrass Festival
November: Día de los Muertos
December: Dance Along Nutcracker

Famous car chase from Bullitt

THE MOVIES

With its unique looks and iconic views, San Francisco has long held an allure for movie-makers, and has played supporting roles in movies of all genres – 1920s silent films, Hitchcock thrillers, sci-fi, and quirky documentaries.

Early moving images were captured in northern California in the late 19th century by Eadweard Muybridge and Thomas Edison, and San Francisco has been a magnet for movie-makers ever since. With its range of romantically iconic views and backdrops. the city has long offered high-value locations for directors. Barbra Streisand deftly maneuvered her Volkswagen between two cable-cars in *What's Up Doc?* (1972); Kim Novak hurled herself from a (non-existent) tower in *Vertigo* (1958) against a backdrop of the Golden Gate Bridge; and Steve McQueen bounced a Mustang over the city's hills in *Bullitt* (1968). More recently, bad mutants inventively used the Golden Gate Bridge against good mutants to win the spectacular battle over a genetic facility located (digitally) on Alcatraz in *X-Men: The Last Stand* (2006) Sean Penn depicted Harvey Milk in *Milk* (2008), and Cate Blanchett played a fallen socialite in *Blue Jasmine* (2013).

A MOVIE-MAKING TRADITION

San Francisco's movie associations date back to the 1920s with the silent movies *The Fog* (1923) and *Greed* (1924). Then came the talkies of the 1930s: Howard Hawks's *Barbary Coast* set in 1850s San Francisco and W.S. Van Dyke's *San Francisco*, which depicted the city collapsing in the 1906 earthquake. In 1941, John Huston's *The Maltese Falcon* had Humphrey Bogart, Peter Lorre, and Sydney Greenstreet skulking in the alleys and backways of Nob Hill. The Fairmont Hotel, atop the same hill, has featured in movies from *Vertigo* in 1958 to *Petulia* (with Julie Christie and George C. Scott) exactly a decade later, to the Sean Connery drama *The Rock* in 1996.

STAR LOCATIONS

Alcatraz (see page 33), of course, has made regular appearances (*The Birdman of Alcatraz*, 1962; *Escape from Alcatraz*, 1979; *The Rock*, 1996), as has City Hall (*The Right Stuff*, 1983; *Class Action*, 1990) and the Golden Gate Bridge (*Superman*, 1978; *A View to a Kill*, 1985; *Interview with the Vampire*, 1994; and many more). The bridge, and Mission Dolores, provided backdrops for *Vertigo*, whose Madeleine Elster (Kim Novak)

Humphrey Bogart in The Maltese Falcon

lives in the Empire Hotel (now Hotel Vertigo) at 940 Sutter Street.

North Beach

The North Beach area is regularly jammed with lights, camera cranes, and trailers. The renowned Saints Peter and Paul Church on Washington Square was the site of a shoot-out in 1971's *Dirty Harry*, and a few blocks away, City Lights Bookstore was the setting for *Flashback*, a 1960s film starring a radical played by Dennis Hopper. The bookstore also featured in the 1980 Beat-inspired movie *Heart Beat* with Nick Nolte, Sissy Spacek, and John Hurt.

The Tosca Café, across the street at 242 Columbus Avenue, featured in *Basic Instinct* (1992), starring Michael Douglas and Sharon Stone, as did the country-and-western bar Rawhide on 7th Street in South of Market.

Downtown

The Bank of America at 555 California Street became "America's tallest skyscraper" in 1974 as 86 fictional stories were added and then torched in Irwin Allen's disaster movie *The Towering Inferno*.

The Transamerica Pyramid, one of the city's most emblematic buildings, has featured in dozens of films, including the 1978 remake of the science-fiction movie *Invasion of the Body Snatchers*, shot by the hometown director Philip Kaufman. With the aid of time-lapse photography, director David Fincher used the pyramid, as well as a number of other buildings that transformed the city's skyline in the 1970s, to dramatic effect by chronicling its rise to convey the passage of time in his 2007 film, *Zodiac*.

LOCAL FILM HEAVYWEIGHTS

"Just say Francis Coppola is up in San Francisco in an old warehouse making films," announced Coppola in 1971. Two years before, he and fellow upstart George Lucas left Hollywood to start their own studio, American Zoetrope. Lucas now has 1,300 employees at his Skywalker Ranch in nearby Nicasio and other Marin County locations. His $2-billion business includes the *Star Wars* movies, *Indiana Jones*, the THX soundsystem, and Industrial Light & Magic. Lucas's San Francisco home is the Letterman Arts campus, in the coveted Presidio near the Golden Gate Bridge.

FILM FESTIVALS

San Francisco hosts numerous film festivals every year. In addition to the San Francisco International Film Festival (http://sffs.org), there's the San Francisco International LGBT Film Festival (www.frameline.org), San Francisco Jewish Film Festival (www.sfjff.org), San Francisco Silent Film Festival (www.silentfilm.org), Noir City (www.noircity.com), and Spike and Mike's Festival of Animation (www.spikeandmike.com).

The city burns following the 1906 earthquake

HISTORY: KEY DATES

San Francisco's early history witnessed European colonialism, the discovery of gold, and an earthquake that changed the face of the city forever. The 1900s saw the influx of beatniks, hippies, yuppies, and, then the dot-com revolution.

EARLY HISTORY

8,000 BC	Ancestors of the Ohlone and Miwok tribes inhabit the sandy plains of what would later become the San Francisco Bay.

SETTLEMENT AND FOUNDING

1579	Sir Francis Drake lands at Port Reyes.
1776	The Spanish arrive and the Misión San Francisco de Asís – now better known as Mission Dolores – is built.
1822	Mexico wins its independence from Spain; California becomes a Mexican territory.
1846	John Montgomery of the U.S.S. *Portsmouth* first raises the Stars and Stripes in present-day Portsmouth Square.
1847	The settlement of Yerba Buena is renamed San Francisco.
1848	Gold is discovered in the Sierra Nevada foothills. The Treaty of Guadalupe Hildago is signed, making California American.
1849	Gold Rush sparks the greatest mass migration in history.
1850	U.S. Congress grants California statehood.
1869	Transcontinental Railroad is completed.
1870	William Hammond Hall begins turning the city's western sand dunes into Golden Gate Park.
1875	Anti-Chinese riots raze Chinatown.

20TH CENTURY

1906	On April 18, an earthquake destroys much of the city and leaves thousands dead or homeless.
1910	Angel Island Immigration Station opens. Known as "the Ellis Island of the West," it will process 175,000 immigrants.

Historic murals at Coit Tower

1915	Panama-Pacific Exposition is hosted in the area later christened the Marina.
1933	Coit Tower is completed.
1937	The Golden Gate Bridge opens, some six months after the Bay Bridge is completed.
1940	The Lower Fillmore jazz clubs attract greats such as Ella Fitzgerald, Duke Ellington, Billie Holiday, Charles Mingus, and Charlie Parker to the "Harlem of the West."
1941–5	Some 1.6 million American military personnel pass through Fort Mason, and the Bay Area's industry booms.
1945	The United Nations charter is signed in the War Memorial Opera House.
1955	Allen Ginsberg reads his poem *Howl* at Gallery Six, igniting the San Francisco Poetry Renaissance.
1957	San Francisco columnist Herb Caen coins the word "Beatnik."
1967	Haight-Ashbury blossoms in the "Summer of Love," making the city the center of the counterculture.
1971	Inspired by the Chicano civil rights movement, artists begin mural series on the Mission's Balmy Alley.
1977	Harvey Milk is elected city supervisor, becoming the first openly gay person elected to public office in the U.S.
1978	Supervisor Harvey Milk and Mayor George Moscone are killed by former Supervisor Dan White.
1989	During the opening of the World Series at Candlestick Park, the 7.1-magnitude Loma Prieta earthquake rocks the Bay Area
1995	The "New Economy" of the flashy dot-com era dominates much of San Francisco life until the bubble bursts in October, 2002.

21ST CENTURY

2000	The San Francisco Giants open the new stadium, now AT&T Park.
2003	200,000 San Franciscans are part of the largest international anti-war demonstration in history.
2004	Mayor Gavin Newsom issues marriage licenses for same-sex couples, putting this controversial issue on the national stage.
2006	San Francisco Representative Nancy Pelosi becomes the first woman elected Speaker of the House of Representatives.
2013	75th anniversary of the Bay Bridge; the new span is opened.

BEST ROUTES

Paddling in the bay

FISHERMAN'S WHARF

Weave through the lively daytime crowds along seaside Fisherman's Wharf for sunbathing sea lions, historic ships, a double-decker carousel, hot-fudge sundaes and tchotchkes galore, then ride a creaky cable-car back downtown.

DISTANCE: 2 miles (3km)

TIME: A half-day

START: Pier 39

END: Ghirardelli Square

POINTS TO NOTE: The piers near Fisherman's Wharf are also the place to catch a ferry to Alcatraz and across the bay. This tour begins at Pier 39 (Powell–Hyde or Powell–Mason cable-car; Metro: F; bus: 39, 47)

Fisherman's Wharf is filled with knick-knack stores, carnivalesque attractions, and scores of tourists, making it easy to forget that it represents the maritime past that is so integral to San Francisco's character. In the maritime present, it is still the place to pick up a ferry to Alcatraz (see page 33) or Angel Island, as well as across the bay. There are also lots of seafood restaurants and pleasant cafés.

If crowds and trinkets hold no appeal, visit the waterfront in the evening when the stores have closed and everyone has gone home. Then, accompanied only by barking sea lions and the city's lights on the bay, it is much easier to enjoy the saltiness of this once-bustling harbor.

PIER 39

Built from old wharves and anchoring the 45-acre (18-hectare) wharf area, **Pier 39 ❶** is a major tourist attraction, second only to Disneyland in California. Young children can ride the hand-painted vintage **San Francisco Carousel**, where traditional leaping horses and rocking chariots circle beneath painted depictions of local landmarks. Weave through the decked plazas filled with kitsch and head to the western side to see and hear the playful squabbles of some of the city's most famed inhabitants: hundreds of boisterous **sea lions ❷**, which hang out on pontoons in the water below. Endearingly known as "Sea Lebrities," the sea lions first arrived in January 1990 as a herd of 10–15, but within a few short months (thanks to the sheltered location and plentiful her-

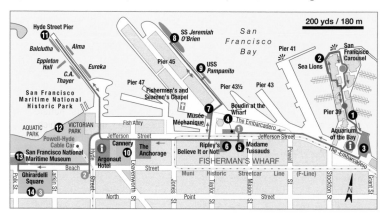

Fisherman's Wharf sign

Several of the city's famous noisy sea lions

ring supply) the small gathering had ballooned to a party of 300. The population peaked at 1,701 in November 2009; now the numbers vary from season to season.

To see more of the bay's sea life, enter the nearby **Aquarium of the Bay** ❸ (Pier 39; www.aquariumofthebay.com; June–Aug: daily 9am–8pm, Sept–May: Mon–Fri 10am–6pm, Sat–Sun 10am–7pm; charge), home to some 20,000 local marine animals. Walk through the underwater glass tunnel to see sharks, fish, and crustaceans from a diver's-eye view.

SEAFOOD AND SOURDOUGH

Walk west on Jefferson Street, the principal thoroughfare of Fisherman's Wharf, traversed by the F-Line's vintage streetcars on their way downtown and home to seafood street vendors hawking boiled shellfish and chowder in an edible sourdough bowl. *Cioppino* is San Francisco's own brand of catch-of-the-day seafood stew. Its name is derived from *ciuppin*, meaning to chop in the Ligurian dialect spoken by the Italian fishermen who first created the dish out of San Francisco Bay's bounty.

For some of San Francisco classic sourdough bread, stop at the flagship **Boudin at the Wharf** ❹, see ❶, which still uses the "starter" yeast culture that Isidore Boudin – son of a family of master bakers from Burgandy – developed during the Gold Rush. Peer through sidewalk windows to see expert bakers working on loaves, baguettes, and more unusual shapes such as lobsters, alligators, and teddy bears. Upstairs, take a self-guided tour

Aquarium of the Bay

of the museum (daily 11.30am–9pm; charge) and observe the bakery in full swing below.

JEFFERSON STREET ATTRACTIONS

This block of Jefferson Street is home two oddball attractions. Across the street from Boudin at No. 145 is **Madame Tussauds** ❺ (www.madametussauds.com; charge), with its rather creepy cast of life-size wax characters. Just a few doors down is **Ripley's Believe It or Not!** ❻ (175 Jefferson Street; www.ripleys.com/sanfrancisco; Sun–Thur 10am–10pm, Fri–Sat 10am–10pm; charge), with its Mona Lisa made of Rubik's cubes, an original vampire-killing kit, and other bizarre curiosities.

PIER 45

Turn right at Taylor Street to reach Pier 45, which along with nearby **Fish Alley** forms the working heart of Fisherman's Wharf. From here, fishermen depart in the before dawn and return midmorning. Their catch is packed and sold in the tin-roofed sheds along Fish Alley. The same fishermen often guide or captain the many bay tours that launch from here in the afternoon. Tucked away amid a network of piers and boats, the tiny Fishermen's and Seamen's Chapel is dedicated to those lost at sea in North California. Once a year, traditionally on the first Sunday of Octo-

ber, there is a ceremony blessing San Francisco's fishing fleet.

Musée Mécanique

At Pier 45's Shed A is the **Musée Mécanique** ❼ (www.museemecanique.org; daily 10am–7pm, Sat–Sun until 8pm; free), an incredible collection of some 300 mechanical relics, some of which formerly operated at Playland, the city's amusement park which closed in 1972. Bring a pocket full of quarters to play with vintage penny-arcade games, antique slot machines, hand-cranked music boxes, coin-operated pianos, and dubious fortune-tellers.

SS Jeremiah O'Brien

Further down Pier 45 is the **SS Jeremiah O'Brien** ❽ (www.ssjeremiahobrien.org; daily 9am–4pm; charge), which can be fully explored from the engine room to the flying bridge. The functional WWII Liberty Ship participated in the D-Day invasion of Normandy, carrying supplies and personnel across the English Channel. Just next to the SS *Jeremiah O'Brien* is the submarine **USS Pampanito** ❾ (tel: 775-1943; www.maritime.org; May–Oct: daily from 9am, call for closing times; charge).

THE CANNERY

Return on Taylor Street and turn right on Jefferson Street. Just after the **Anchorage Hotel**, pass the redbrick **Cannery** ❿ (Jefferson and Leavenworth streets;

Bubba Gump Shrimp Co.

US Navy ship moored at Pier 45

www.delmontesquare.com; hours vary between businesses). Now a shopping center, this was formerly the Del Monte cannery, once the largest fruit and vegetable cannery in the world.

HYDE STREET PIER

Continue west on Jefferson Sreet and turn right on Hyde Street. The **Hyde Street Pier** ⑪ was the original Ferry terminal for Sausalito and Berkeley, and is home to the **Hyde Street Pier Historic Ships Collection** (www.nps. gov/safr; daily 9.30am–5pm; charge). The pier is part of the National Maritime Park, the country's smallest national park. Its Visitor Center is located across the street in the **Argonaut Hotel** (499 Jefferson Street; tel: 447-5000).

Moored along the pier are vintage vessels built in the late 19th and early 20th centuries. Tour below decks of the steam-driven *Eureka*, which was built in 1890 and is the last of 50 paddle-wheel ferries that transported passengers between San Francisco and Tiburon before the bay's bridges were built. See how to set the topsail and staysail on board the *Balclutha*, a steel-hulled Scottish square-rigger built in 1886 that made 17 journeys around Cape Horn before its final voyage in 1930. Time your visit right and you can also raise your voice to the tune of sailor songs at the monthly Chantey Sing (tel: 561-7171; 1st Saturday of month 8pm–midnight; reservations required). The other

historic ships on site are two schooners, a steam tug, and a paddlewheel tug.

Walk south on Hyde Street toward Beach Street. You will pass **Victorian Park** ⑫ on the left, frequently filled with people waiting for the **Powell-Hyde cable-car** line that ends here. Just past Beach Street, break for a legendary Irish coffee at **Buena Vista Café** ❷.

AQUATIC PARK AND SAN FRANCISCO NATIONAL MARITIME MUSEUM

Walk west along Beach Street, overlooking **Aquatic Park** whose pleasant urban beach and romantic promenade lead to the **Municipal Pier** and on to **Fort Mason** (see page 84) one of the city's earliest military installations that dates back to the 1850s.

Perched above Aquatic Park is the **San Francisco National Maritime Museum** ⑬ (900 Beach Street; www.nps.gov/safr; daily 10am–4pm, free). Built during the 1930s with the rest of Aquatic Park, it resembles a beached ocean liner in the Art Deco style of its day. It was commissioned by the federal government as one of the Works Progress Administration projects in the 1930s, a major relief measure that was established to create jobs for the many unemployed people in the city at the time. The museum celebrates San Francisco's colorful maritime heritage with interactive exhibits, intricate models, muralist Hilaire Hiler's 1930s expressionist vision of Atlantis,

Ghirardelli's chocolate emporium

Food and Drink

① BOUDIN AT THE WHARF

160 Jefferson Street; tel: 928-1849; www.boudinbakery.com; daily B, L, and D; $

The flagship location is the perfect spot to try the tangy-flavored sourdough bread that the company began baking back in 1849. Nosh on classic sandwiches and soups in indoor and outdoor seating. Upstairs is the fancier Bistro Boudin (tel: 351-5561; daily L and D; $$$) for upscale pastas, seafood, and entrées.

② BUENA VISTA CAFÉ

2765 Hyde Street; tel: 474-5044; www.thebuenavista.com; daily B, L, and D; $$

A San Francisco institution and home of the legendary Irish coffee, a delicious elixir made with Irish whiskey, frothed cream, and coffee. The recipe was whipped up in 1952 in response to a challenge made by writer Stan Delaplane, and is still served in steaming chalices to up to 2,000 happy drinkers each day.

③ GHIRARDELLI CHOCOLATE ICE CREAM AND CHOCOLATE SHOP

Ghirardelli Square at Larkin; tel: 474-3938; www.ghirardelli.com; Sun–Thur 9am–11pm, Fri–Sat 9am–midnight; $

With a separate ice cream fountain that opens at 10am every day, this is a tried-and-true spot for ice cream, hot fudge, and all things chocolate.

oral history recreations, and scores of other sea-faring memorabilia, from tools to artifacts to photographs.

GHIRARDELLI SQUARE

Cross Beach Street to end your day at **Ghirardelli Square** ⑭ (900 North Point Street; www.ghirardellisq.com), the proud recipient of city, state, and federal landmark status. A small shopping center capped by a 15ft (4m) illuminated sign, Ghirardelli Square is named after Domingo Ghirardelli, an Italian merchant who settled in San Francisco in 1849 and opened the original Ghirardelli Chocolate Factory just 13 days before the gold discovery at Sutter's Mill that led to the Gold Rush. Focus on the dessert options here, especially the decadent sundaes at **Ghirardelli Chocolate Ice Cream and Chocolate Shop** ③.

POWELL–HYDE CABLE-CAR

The tour ends here, but a great way to return downtown is via quintessential San Francisco transportation: the cable-car. Return to Larkin and Beach streets and then wait in line for the Powell–Hyde service, which runs through Russian Hill's leafy Hyde Street, over Nob Hill's hair-raising slopes, along the edge of Chinatown, and down to Union Square. The cable-cars generally depart every 10–20 minutes from 6am to 1am (at time of printing a single ticket was $6, an all-day pass $15).

Alcatraz cell block

ALCATRAZ

Hop on a ferry to explore the famous cell blocks of Alcatraz, the Disneyland of the world's former prison islands. Where once infamous criminals were incarcerated, the island now sees more than 1.4 million visitors each year and is the most visited attraction in San Francisco.

DISTANCE: Less than 1 mile (2km)
TIME: 3 hours
START/END: Pier 33
POINTS TO NOTE: Book tickets as far in advance as possible; tel: 981-7625; tours: www.alcatrazcruises.com; daily 8.45am (first ferry out), 4.30pm (last ferry back, unless taking a night tour); charge; Metro: F to Embarcadero and Bay Street.

Tales of The Rock have fascinated Americans since the golden years of the American gangster. Now operated by the National Parks Service, anyone can come and go to Alcatraz not just to explore the prison, but also the island's unique flora and fauna.

Early history

Alcatraz was christened *La Isla de los Alcatraces* (the island of the pelicans) by Spanish explorers in 1775. Originally built as a military garrison, Alcatraz was prized for its strategic significance. Its position in the bay made it ideal for use as a defensive and disciplinary facility, and by the mid-1800s, US Army soldiers stood guard. It became a prison in 1895, when Modoc and Hopi tribe leaders were imprisoned there. Responding to the crime wave sweeping the country in the 1920s and 1930s, the government decided Alcatraz was sufficiently fortified to house the most violent offenders, and took over the prison in 1934.

Federal penitentiary

Somber by day and eerily illuminated at night, Alcatraz is a haunting presence in the San Francisco Bay. For prisoners of The Rock, the sounds of the city, from the clang of the cable-cars to the light echoes of evening cocktail parties, would float across the water into their cells as haunting reminders of the world outside.

The prisoners in those cell blocks were once some of the most hardened criminals of the 20th century, including Chicago mob boss Al Capone, bootlegger George "Machine Gun" Kelly, and Robert Shroud (played by

The Rock as seen from the air

Burt Lancaster in the film *The Birdman of Alcatraz*).

Prison cells were designed for maximum security. Just 5ft by 9ft (1.5m by 3m), inmates had to spend 16 to 23 hours a day in them. Alcatraz Federal Penitentiary quickly gained a reputation for its harsh system of earned privileges for the most basic rights, its deadening solitary confinement, and the cold, damp weather. Just three privileges were available to the best-behaved inmates: the recreation yard, the library, or a job in one of the on-site factories.

Guards and their families lived on the island and considered it to be so safe that they rarely locked their doors.

No escape

Escape from Alcatraz required a treacherous 1.5-mile (2.5km) swim to San Francisco. Of 36 attempted escapes, none are known to have succeeded: of these 23 were caught alive, six were shot and killed during their escape, two drowned, and five were presumed drowned. In 1963, Attorney General Robert Kennedy closed the crumbling and expensive prison, and it was turned over to the National Park Service. A replacement facility opened in Illinois.

Indian occupation

Six years later, a large group of Native Americans under the banner "Indians of All Tribes" occupied the island until 1971. Protesting against the many treaties with Native Americans that had been broken by the U.S. government, the group claimed Alcatraz as well as funds to build an Indian center and university. While the occupation ended with no demands met, it jump-started the Pan-Indian Movement and prompted the U.S. government to adopt a policy of Indian self-determination. Lasting reminders of the occupation include the burned-out shell of the warden's house destroyed by a 1970 fire, a blaze the group was unable to extinguish as the government had cut off their only water source a few weeks before.

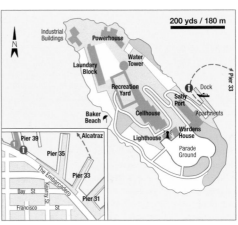

A cramped prison cell *The Power House supplied electricity to buildings on the island*

VISITING THE PARK

A ferry service to the island departs from Pier 33, roughly every half-hour from 8.45am–1.35pm and takes about 10–15 minutes each way; return ferries run until 4.30pm. It is advised to allow at least 2.5 hours for the entire trip. Tickets (which can be purchased online, by phone, or at Pier 33) are expensive, but cover the transit cost and the 45-minute Cellhouse Audio Tour. Popular Night Tours are also available (Thur–Mon 4.30pm; charge), with a narrated boat tour around the island, guided island tours, and a variety of special activities. During the summer, on weekends, and holidays tickets should be purchased in advance.

Both the island and the ferry ride to it can be plagued by cold and foggy weather, regardless of the time of year. Wear layers and comfortable walking shoes to negotiate the uneven walkways and steep, uphill climb from the dock to the main level. For more information visit http://www.parksconservancy.org/visit/tours/alcatraz.html and www.nps.gov/alcatraz.

On the island

Somber by day and eerily illuminated at night, Alcatraz is a haunting presence in the bay. Once on the island, ask park rangers for assistance and information regarding tours. The cells and notorious Segregation Unit can be viewed; there is also a museum, two bookstores, and a visitor center located both on the dock and at the main level. Child-friendly programs are available along with guided walks through the island's gardens and natural landscape, which offers a rare and unique variety of plant, animal, and bird life. Recently, the Alcatraz Historic Gardens Project rebuilt the gardens and natural landscape surrounding the prison. Once tended by inmates and prison personnel as a popular pastime, these gardens provided color, as well as hope and reprieve from the harsh world behind the penitentiary's locked doors.

Also note the island's lighthouse; built in 1854, it was the first lighthouse on the bay.

Back on the mainland

Food is not available on the island, so bring refreshments or head to Pier 39 when you return for a bite at the **Eagle Café ❶**.

Food and Drink

❶ EAGLE CAFÉ
Pier 39; tel: 433-3689; www.eaglecafe.com; daily B, L, and D; $
A great alternative to many higher-priced Fisherman's Wharf restaurants, the Eagle is a lively institution known for large portions, hearty breakfasts, stiff cocktails, and stellar views.

Vesuvio Café

NORTH BEACH AND TELEGRAPH HILL

Vibrant North Beach is a lively mix of Italian trattorias, laid-back cafés, bars crammed with 20-something revellers, and a crowd of strip clubs on Broadway. Nearby Telegraph Hill offers stunning 360-degree views at Coit Tower.

DISTANCE: 2 miles (3km)
TIME: A half-day
START: Jackson Square
END: Levi's Plaza
POINTS TO NOTE: Stairways render the final portion of this route, from Coit Tower onwards, inaccessible by wheelchair. The route starts at Jackson Square, at Pacific and Montgomery (BART and Metro: Embarcadero and Montgomery stations; bus: 30, 45). If you're traveling with children and would like to visit the Exploratorium in the morning, try this route in reverse.

North Beach is a neighborhood best known for its excesses – in literature, food, libations, and sex. It is where you can find the ghosts of the city's famed Beat past and the best espresso in the city, with the area's early-1900s Italian roots still much in evidence.

Despite its name, North Beach borders no water – its name was chosen at a time when the bay extended roughly to today's Bay Street. Nearby Telegraph

Hill, which has always been a part of, and yet apart from, North Beach, was largely ignored by early settlers, who preferred to fill in the shallows of the bay below rather than build on the hill itself. Irish stevedores were some of the earliest inhabitants of the hill, using the rickety network of stairs to get to and from work and the docks every day. They were replaced by Italian immigrants, then later by bohemians, who liked the views and seclusion. Today, real estate around Telegraph Hill – full of charm and heart-stopping vistas – is among the most desirable in San Francisco.

NORTH BEACH

Start the route at **Jackson Square** ❶, one of the best remaining enclaves of mid-19th-century San Francisco. Built in the 1850s, the brick architecture that surrounds it was one of the lucky few buildings in the area to withstand the 1906 earthquake and the following fire. The earthquake totally destroyed North Beach, but it was quickly rebuilt, though with few of the architectural flourishes for

City Lights Bookstore   *A bookworm's delight and Beatnik haunt*

which the city is famous. These understated Victorian and Edwardian buildings came to be known as "1906 specials."

Despite its chic galleries, antiques stores, design studios, and quaint, tree-lined ambience, this quiet neighborhood was a place of unparalled vice during the Gold Rush. The Barbary Coast (as it was then called) was a vast marketplace of flesh and liquor. Sailors and miners found fleeting pleasures, fast money, and, just as likely, a faster end. Second to gambling, shoot-outs were the favored sport, and fortunes rode on the wink of an eye. Most businessmen in the Barbary Coast trafficked in human bodies: either selling sex to '49ers or selling drugged and kidnapped sailors to the captains of ships headed to China (a practice that became known as "shanghaiing." Both enterprises returned high profits, and local politicians turned a blind eye for a piece of the action. Red lights burned on almost every block, from both high-class "parlors" and squalid "cribs," where prostitutes worked in rooms barely big enough to hold a bed. In the worst cases, Chinese girls were bought as slaves and made to work until they became sick or died.

Columbus Avenue

Walk west on Jackson Street and turn right onto Columbus Avenue. This intersection hosts the flatiron **Sentinel Building** ❷ at 916 Kearny Street, restored by film director and producer Francis Ford Coppola in the 1970s. It is now home to Coppola's production company, Amer-

ican Zoetrope Studios, which counts *Apocalypse Now*, *American Graffiti*, and *Lost in Translation* among its films. Columbus is North Beach's dominant commercial street, filled with delis, restaurants, and cafés that spill onto the sidewalks. Another main thoroughfare is narrow Grant Avenue, home to family-run Italian businesses and a hot spot of the North Beach nightlife scene.

City Lights Bookstore

After World War II, rents in North Beach were low, the jazz and coffeehouse scenes lively, and the neighborhood's character lascivious; the area became the West Coast hub of Beat poets, writers, and artists. Among them were Jack Kerouac, Allen Ginsberg, Gary Snyder, Lawrence Ferlinghetti, Philip Whalen, and Michael McClure. This heritage is still visible at **City Lights Bookstore** ❸ (261 Columbus Avenue; www.citylights.com; daily 10am–midnight) a left-leaning "Beatnikdom" cornerstone that was co-founded by Ferlinghetti and is now a National Literary Landmark. Also a publisher, City Lights gained notoriety in 1956 by publishing Allen Ginsburg's poem *Howl* and winning the obscenity case that was brought against the company.

Vesuvio Café

Next door to City Lights sits **Vesuvio Café** ❹ (255 Columbus Avenue; www.vesuvio.com; daily 6am–2am), a cool Beatnik haunt frequented by everyone from Bob

North Beach music store

Dylan to Dylan Thomas. Here, Jack Kerouac was famously "delayed" one night in 1960 when he was scheduled to meet novelist Henry Miller in Big Sur. Between Vesuvio and City Lights is **Jack Kerouac Alley**, one of several city streets honoring local literati. The truly Beat-obsessed can turn right at Broadway for the **Beat Museum ⑤** (540 Broadway Street; www.kerouac.com; daily 10am–7pm; charge), which displays a handful of books, photographs, letters, and other memorabilia and hosts occasional events including poetry and book readings.

Red-light district

The intersection of **Columbus, Broadway and Grant ⑥** gamely carries on the Barbary Coast's red-light tradition with strip-clubs, adult video parlors, and racy late-night clubs, including the **Hungry I** (546 Broadway Street), which helped launch the careers of big names such as Woody Allen and Bill Cosby. Carol Doda made history at the **Condor Club** (300 Columbus Avenue) performing the first topless (1964) then bottomless (1969) act in the country, while descending from the ceiling on top of a piano.

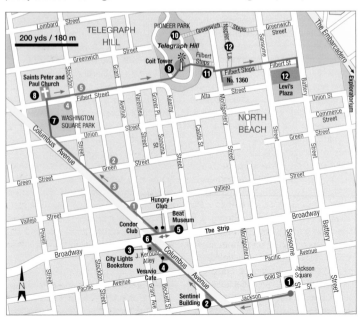

The Hungry I   *Victorian architecture in North Beach*

At Grant and Vallejo, stop at the West Coast's home of the espresso, **Caffe Trieste** ❶. This was another Beatnik hang and allegedly where Coppola wrote his screenplay for *The Godfather*. If you're craving something heavier, **Golden Boy Pizza** is close by ❷, or for a sweet treat, visit **Stella's Pastry and Café** ❸.

Washington Square

Continue along Columbus and escape from North Beach's congested streets into **Washington Square Park** ❼, where everyone from elderly Italians and Chinese tai chi devotees to flirting sunbathers and shirtless Frisbee-throwers congregate on warm weekends. The life-sized Ben Franklin statue dates from 1879 and is the oldest existing monument in San Francisco. The statue was a gift to the city from H.D. Cogswell, an eccentric dentist who amassed a fortune by putting gold into miners' teeth – a sign of status in a town that worshipped the shiny metal.

Saints Peter and Paul Church

Across Filbert Street are the picturesque Romanesque façade and soaring twin white spires of **Saints Peter and Paul Church** ❽ (666 Filbert Street; www.sspeterpaulsf.org/church; daily 7am–4pm, Sat–Sun until 6pm; free). Built in 1924, the Catholic church holds Mass each day in Italian, Chinese, and English, and is popular for traditional Italian weddings. Baseball legend Joe DiMaggio and his bride Marilyn Monroe even snapped

photos here. The church's many silver-screen credits include Cecil B. DeMille's *The Ten Commandments* (1956) and Don Siegel's *Dirty Harry* (1971). Above the main entrance is an inscription from the first canto of Dante's *Paradiso*: "La Gloria Di Colui Che Tutto Muove Per L'Universo Penetra E Risplende" (The glory of Him who moves all things shines throughout the universe).

Before climbing Telegraph Hill, have brunch at **Mama's** ❹ or grab perhaps the city's best focaccia at the **Liguria Bakery** ❺.

TELEGRAPH HILL

If your energy is dwindling, catch the 39 bus to reach **Coit Tower** ❾ (Telegraph Hill Boulevard; daily 10am–6.30pm; charge). Otherwise climb Filbert Street to the east to reach the 210ft (64m) landmark. Surrounded by Pioneer Park, Coit Tower crowns **Telegraph Hill** ❿, so named in 1849 when it became the site of the first telegraph on the West Coast. The tower is a monument to city firefighters, and was erected in 1933 at the bequest of volunteer firefighter and North Beach eccentric, Lillie Hitchcock Coit. Inside are murals in the style of the Mexican artist Diego Rivera, and dazzling 360-degree views can be enjoyed from the top.

Filbert Steps and Napier Lane

Outside, look for the **Filbert Steps** ⓫ to the right (on the left are the **Green-**

View towards Telegraph Hill and Coit Tower

wich Steps) and descend the wooden staircases surrounded by cool, shady gardens. When you reach Montgomery Street, detour to the right briefly to see **1360 Montgomery**, a four-story Art Deco building that starred in the Humphrey Bogart film *Dark Passage* (1947). Continue down the Filbert Steps, passing **Napier Lane** ⑫ on the left, the last wooden plank street left in the city.

Levi's Plaza

From Filbert Street turn right on Battery Street to head back to North Beach; continue until you reach the red bricks and grassy knolls of **Levi's Plaza** ⑬, home of the headquarters of the blue jeans experts Levi Strauss. Across the Embarcadero from Levi's Plaza is one of the best attractions in the city for children, the **Exploratorium** (3601 Lyon Street; tel: 561-0360; www.exploratorium.edu; Tue–Sun 10am–5pm, Thur also 6–10pm for adults; charge). Conceived by the American physicist Frank Oppenheimer, this museum of science, art, and human perception explores topics as varied as physics, computers, biology, visual perception, language, and memory.

Food and Drink

① CAFFE TRIESTE
601 Vallejo Street; tel: 392-6739; www.caffetrieste.com; daily 6.30am–10pm (Fri–Sat until 11pm); $
This quintessentially San Francisco coffeehouse claims to be the first place on the West Coast to serve espresso back in the 1950s. Cash only.

② GOLDEN BOY PIZZA
542 Green Street; tel: 982-9738; daily L and D; $
Golden Boy's Sicilian-style pan pizza is a favorite of North Beach bar-goers, and usually ordered by the slice.

③ STELLA'S PASTRY AND CAFÉ
466 Columbus Avenue; tel: 986-2194; daily

B, L, and D; bus: 30, 41, 45; $
Try the *sacripantina* (a divine creamy layered cake laced with liquor) or the mouthwatering tiramisu at this beloved bakery.

④ MAMA'S
1701 Stockton Street; tel: 362-6421; www.mamas-sf.com; Tue–Sun B and L; $
The line is crazy on weekends at this legendary brunch spot, so either be waiting when they open at 8am, come on a weekday, or try the afternoon.

⑤ LIGURIA BAKERY
1700 Stockton Street; tel: 421-3786; Mon–Fri 8am–2pm, Sat 7am–2pm, Sun 7am–noon (closes earlier if they sell out); $
You just haven't had focaccia till you've had a slice of Liguria's, but come early because it sells out quickly.

Kong Chow Temple

CHINATOWN

Amble through Chinatown's animated streets and alleys, which buzz with commotion and are peppered with produce stands, purveyors of fortune cookies, tiny temples, dried herbs, dim sum, and swarms of souvenirs.

DISTANCE: 1 mile (2km)
TIME: 3 hours
START/END: Chinatown Gate
POINTS TO NOTE: Visit during normal business hours when the streets are most alive. This route begins at the intersection of Bush Street and Grant Avenue near Union Square (BART and Metro: Montgomery or Powell Street stations; bus: Market Street lines).

San Francisco's Chinatown is one of those rare tourist attractions that is also a dynamic community. It is as close as you can get to a city within a city, complete with its own banks, schools, doctors, and sweatshops, sadly reminiscent of those at the turn of the 20th century.

Historic hub

Despite Chinatown's being in a sense a world of its own, it has been a significant part of San Francisco's history since the earliest days of the Gold Rush. Due to the political upheaval and widespread famine in Southern China in the 1850s, thousands of Chinese came to California to find their fortunes in the goldfields of the Sierras or to work on the Transcontinental Railroad. These immigrants quickly set up a commercial district near the then center of town, Portsmouth Square.

By the mid-19th century, "Little Canton," as it was then known, was filled with hotels, boarding houses, restaurants, stores, and pharmacies plying herbal remedies. Christened "Chinatown" by the local press, it was also notorious as a magnet for vice. Brothels, opium dens, and gambling rings were legion and often exaggerated to justify rampant anti-Chinese racism.

Discrimination and hostility reached a boiling point in the aftermath of the 1906 earthquake and fire, which leveled the ramshackle Chinatown. Seeing the opportunity to seize the valuable downtown real estate, as well as to eradicate what they saw as a blight on the city, San Francisco's leaders attempted to relocate Chinatown to the distant southeast corner of the city.

Chinatown Gate

However, the residents of Chinatown would have no such thing, and due to their steadfastness and the intervention of the Dowager Empress on behalf of her distant subjects, Chinatown was rebuilt in its original spot in the heart of the city. In recent years, the city's Chinese population has grown substantially in other areas including the Richmond, Sunset and Russian Hill neighborhoods. Yet, with 100,000 residents packed into just 24 square blocks, Chinatown remains the thriving cultural heart of the Bay Area's Chinese community.

Chinese New Year

Every year in early spring, Chinatown sees the biggest Chinese New Year's celebration outside of Asia, cramming thousands into the neighborhood for festivities. Firecracker wrappers litter every alleyway, vendors fill the streets, and a spectacular parade with a 201ft (61m) Golden Dragon is the high point of the celebration.

CHINATOWN GATE AND GRANT AVENUE

The "official" entrance of Chinatown is through the ornate Chinatown Gate, or "**Dragon's Gate**", ❶ that arches over Grant Avenue. Gifted by Taiwan in 1970, the green, dragon-crested structure was modeled after a traditional village gate. At the top of the gate, four gilded Chinese characters in raised relief translate as "Everything in the World is in Just Proportion." Together with Bush Street, it marks the southern edge of Chinatown; the western, northern, and eastern borders are marked by Powell, Broadway, and Kearny streets, respectively.

Pass underneath the gate along Grant Avenue, the oldest street in San Francisco. First named in 1845 by the town of Yerba Buena as Calle de la Fundación, it also served a long stint as Dupont Street, in honor of an admiral of the U.S.S. *Portsmouth*. Grant Avenue is one of Chinatown's most vital arteries. Racks of tourist-targeting merchandise spill onto sidewalks overwhelmed with silks, satiny slippers, teapots, carved teak, jade, jewelry, and other Chinese tchotchkes (souvenirs or knick-knacks).

Dragon House

A respite is offered by the authentic **Dragon House** ❷ (455 Grant Avenue; daily 10am–6pm) and its genuine Asian antiques and fine arts. Though Grant Avenue feels in many ways like a Disney version of "Chinatown," do not be fooled: behind the tourist-oriented commercialism exists a thriving, insular, and in many ways impenetrable community.

ST MARY'S SQUARE

From Grant Avenue, turn right onto Pine Street. The entrance to **St Mary's**

Bilingual street sign　　　　　　　　　　　　　*Old St Mary's Church*

Square ❸ (daily 6am–10pm) is on the left. In this small but peaceful patch of refuge from the busy surrounding streets, Chinatown residents and Financial District workers on lunch breaks rest on wooden benches.

Note the large metal-and-granite statue designed by Beniamino Bufano; the statue honors reformer Dr. Sun Yatsen, a leader of the rebellion that ended the Qing Dynasty's reign and helped to establish the Republic of China in the early 1900s.

OLD ST MARY'S CHURCH

Exit the square heading north and cross California Street to reach the Roman Catholic **Old St Mary's Church ❹** (660 California Street; www.oldsaintmarys. org; Mon–Fri 7am–4.30pm, Sat 7am–6pm, Sun 7am–3pm; free). Established in 1853, this Paulist-led parish church was California's first cathedral and San Francisco's Catholic cathedral for most of the second half of the 19th century. Eventually its location amidst neighbors of ill repute (note the inscription outside beneath the clock that reads "Son Observe the Time and Fly from Evil") led to the construction of a new cathedral at a better-respected address. Although the building survived the 1906 earthquake, it was gutted by the ensuing fire and rebuilt in 1909.

NICHE SHOPS

Turn right onto Grant Avenue and continue north for some of Chinatown's unique shops. (If you need a pitstop at this point, pop into the **Eastern Bakery ❶**, at No. 720.) The **Chinatown Kite Shop ❺** (717 Grant Avenue; www.

Passing a mural on Ross Street

chinatownkite.com; daily 9.30am–9pm) is a kaleidoscope of kites in every shape and size and is crammed with phoenixes, dragons, butterflies, and more. Across the street, the **Wok Shop** ❻ (718 Grant Avenue; tel: 989-3797; www.wokshop.com; daily 10am–6pm) dispenses woks, sake sets, sushi-making tools, and a melting pot of everything else you could want for Chinese cooking adventures.

PORTSMOUTH SQUARE

From Grant Avenue, turn right onto Clay Street to reach **Portsmouth Square** ❼. Designed in 1839, this Chinatown community gathering place is steeped in history and often considered the birthplace of San Francisco. The square was once the town center of Yerba Buena, and overlooked Yerba Buena Cove to the east, where the Financial District skyscrapers stand today. In 1846, this was where Captain John Montgomery of the U.S.S. *Portsmouth* first raised the American flag, and a year later, it was the site of San Francisco's first school (a memorial in the square commemorates the event). Here also Sam Brannan, owner of San Francisco's first newspaper, the *California Star*, announced that gold had been discovered in the Sierra foothills.

Note the 600lb (272kg) bronze *Goddess of Democracy* statue created by volunteers led by sculptor Thomas Marsh. This is a smaller replica of the statue created during the Tiananmen Square protests of 1989.

In the northwest corner of the square is a tribute to writer Robert Louis Stevenson designed by Bruce Porter. In 1879–80, Stevenson came here to ship-watch while waiting for his darling to divorce; today, idlers still flock to chat and people-watch, as youngsters clamber on jungle gyms and old men argue about politics while playing checkers and mah-jong at small tables that dot the square.

CULTURE CENTER

Use the short pedestrian bridge on the eastern edge of the square to enter the **Chinese Culture Center** ❽ (3rd floor; 750 Kearny Street; www.c-c-c.org; Tue–Sat 10am–4pm; free) inside the Hilton San Francisco Financial District. This non-profit organization teaches about historical and modern practices and celebrations in Chinese and Chinese-American culture. Retrace your steps along the pedestrian bridge and exit the square on the north onto Washington Street.

UNITED COMMERCIAL BANK

Head west on Washington Street. On the left is one of Chinatown's original buildings, the **East West Bank** ❾ (743 Washington Street). The three-tiered, pagoda-like structure was built in 1909 after the original was destroyed in the 1906 earthquake. California's first newspaper, the *Cal-

Fortune cookies

Waverly Place, "the street of painted balconies"

ifornia Star, was once printed here, but the building is better known as the one-time home of the Pacific Telephone and Telegraph Company's Chinese Telephone Exchange. In operation from 1894–1949, the telephone exchange was staffed by astonishingly capable female telephone operators. They not only spoke English and five Chinese dialects, but also memorized all the customers' names, as it was considered rude to refer to a person as a number. Moreover, they distinguished between people with the same name by memorizing addresses and job titles!

TOWARDS STOCKTON STREET

Turn north at Grant and continue until Broadway, taking time for a bite to eat at one of the several local options, such as the **Golden Gate Bakery** ② or **Empress of China** ③. Then check out where locals stock up for dinner by walking up Pacific Avenue and then turning left onto bustling **Stockton Street**. This is Chinatown's working center, crammed with Chinese-owned and operated businesses, countless dollar stores, and open-air fresh produce stands and markets.

GOLDEN GATE FORTUNE COOKIE FACTORY

Follow the scent of fresh fortune cookies and turn left onto Jackson Street and then right into the tiny Ross Alley, where the **Golden Gate Fortune Cookie Factory** ⑩ (56 Ross Alley; daily 8am–8pm; free, small charge for taking photographs) has been producing cookie-encased predictions and words of wisdom since 1962. Watch the two workers take flat rounds off the press, stick a fortune inside, and fold them over a rod. Then taste some novelty flat and fortune-less almond or chocolate cookies, bags of which are also for sale.

TIN HOU TEMPLE

Continue south on Ross and cross Washington Street to enter **Waverly Place**, an alley that may sound familiar to fans of Amy Tan's novel set in Chinatown, *The Joy Luck Club*. Known as the "Street of Painted Balconies," Waverly offers a brief reprieve from Chinatown's frenetic hum, with stores selling "real" Chinese goodies, such as lychee wine, pickled ginger, and herbal remedies.

At No. 125, climb up three floors to reach the historic **Tin Hou Temple** ⑪ (daily 10am–4pm; donation suggested), believed to be the oldest Chinese temple in the country. Red paper lanterns blanket the ceiling and incense fills the air inside this tiny temple dedicated to the Queen of the Heavens and Goddess of the Seven Seas, a protector of travelers, sailors, artists, and prostitutes, appropriately enough.

Offerings at the Tin Hou Temple

CHINESE HISTORICAL SOCIETY OF AMERICA

At the junction of Waverly Place and Clay Street, turn right to visit the **Chinese Historical Society of America** ⑫ (965 Clay Street; www.chsa.org; Tue–Fri noon–5pm, Sat 11am–4pm; charge, 1st Thur of month free). At this museum and learning center, small displays explore Chinese-American history, art, and culture, including how Chinese contributions fueled the development of industries in the American West. Note that there is a wheelchair-accessible entrance on Joice Street.

BACK TO CHINATOWN GATE

Walk south on Joice, noting the dark, clinker-brick building on the corner at 920 Sacramento Street. This is the **Donaldina Cameron House** ⑬, designed by the notable San Francisco-born architect Julia Morgan (1872–1957). At this point turn left on Sacramento to browse Chinese and world musical instruments at **Clarion Music Center** ⑭ (816 Sacramento Street; www.clarionmusic.com; Mon–Fri 11am–6pm, Sat 9am–5pm). Then turn right on Grant, passing the atmospheric **Far East Café** ❹, on your return to Chinatown Gate.

Food and Drink

❶ EASTERN BAKERY
720 Grant Avenue; tel: 433-7973; www.easternbakery.com; daily B, L, and D; $
Billed as the oldest Chinese bakery in the U.S. (it opened in 1924), this slightly shabby spot is good for a quick pork bun or some traditional Chinese pastries called mooncakes.

❷ GOLDEN GATE BAKERY
1029 Grant Avenue; tel: 781-2627; daily B, L, and D; $
Beloved of locals, this bakery keeps the crowds happy with traditional treats. Try the egg custards.

❸ EMPRESS OF CHINA
838 Grant Avenue; tel: 434-1345; daily L and D; $
The only restaurant in Chinatown with a truly spectacular view gives diners a very good perspective on the neighborhood. The cocktail lounge overlooks Grant Street, while the dining room towers above Portsmouth Square. If you do not eat here, at least stop by for a drink and enjoy the ambience.

❹ FAR EAST CAFÉ
631 Grant Avenue; tel: 982-3245; daily L and D; $
The food here is good, but the atmosphere is the real draw – some of the best in Chinatown with private booths and century-old chandeliers.

Union Square

SOUTH OF MARKET AND UNION SQUARE

Pick and choose from a smorgasbord of museums and shops on this downtown walk. There's everything from modern art, cartoon art, and historical museums to designer outposts and massive department stores.

DISTANCE: 2 miles (3km)
TIME: A half-day (or more depending on number of museums visited)
START: Cartoon Art Museum
END: Westfield San Francisco Shopping Centre
POINTS TO NOTE: It is not intended for you to visit all the museums on this walk (to do so would be exhausting), so choose a few that particularly catch your interest. This tour begins in the South of Market (SoMa) neighborhood (BART and Metro: Montgomery Street station; bus: 30, 45, Market Street routes).

Begin this tour on Mission Street between Second and Third streets, in the South of Market neighborhood. Once better-known as "South of the Slot" and, in more recent years as SoMa, South of Market is a sprawling district with wide traffic-filled streets stacked with tall office buildings, condo high-rises, hotels, nightclubs, and major museums. Three blocks north of Market Street is Union Square, the heart of the eponymous district famous for upscale stores and top-end hotels.

CARTOON ART MUSEUM

Endowed by *Peanuts* cartoon-strip creator Charles M. Schulz, the **Cartoon Art Museum** ❶ (655 Mission Street; http://cartoon art.org; Tue–Sun 11am–5pm; charge, 1st Tue of month is "Pay What You Wish Day") showcases original cartoons and animation art of both underground and mainstream varieties. Rotating exhibits draw from a permanent collection of 6,000 pieces that range from graphic novels and comic strips to political and advertising cartoons.

MUSEUM OF THE AFRICAN DIASPORA (MOAD)

Walk southeast toward Third Street along Mission street to reach the **Museum of the African Diaspora (MoAD)** ❷ (685 Mission Street; www. moadsf.org; Wed–Sat 11am–6pm,

California Historical Society Museum

Sun noon–5pm; charge). The artwork and artifacts on exhibit focus on the global, uniting influence of the art, culture, and history of Africa. Permanent displays showcase rituals and ceremony, slavery passages, music, theater, adornment, and culinary traditions, and are supplemented with varied rotating exhibits.

CALIFORNIA HISTORICAL SOCIETY

Just across the street from MoAD is the **California Historical Society Museum** ❸ (678 Mission Street; www.california historicalsociety.org; Tue–Sat noon–5pm; charge). In this museum, early California history is chronicled by 5,000 oil paintings, drawings, costumes, lithographs, and decorative arts. There is also an important collection of 500,000 photographs, including works by Eadweard Muybridge and Ansel Adams, and a good gift shop.

SAN FRANCISCO MUSEUM OF MODERN ART (SFMOMA)

Turn left on Third Street to reach the **San Francisco Museum of Modern Art** ❹ (Closed for expansion until 2016; 151 Third Street; www.sfmoma. org). Designed by internationally renowned Swiss architect Mario Botta, the SFMOMA building is marked by a truncated tower with black-and-white bands. The museum's permanent collection is strong in American Abstract Expressionism, Fauvism, and German Expressionism. One of its most well known works is Henri Matisse's seminal *Femme au chapeau (Woman with the Hat)*, painted in 1905. Other painting highlights include Jackson Pollock's *Guardians of the Secret* (1943), René Magritte's 1952 *Les Valeurs personnelles (Personal Values)*, and works by Paul Klee, Piet Mondrian, Pablo Picasso, Andy Warhol, and Georgia O'Keeffe. Diego Rivera's bold, bright *Cargador de flores (The Flower Carrier*, 1935) is complemented by Frida Kahlo's *Frida y Diego Rivera* (1931).

Sculptural highlights include Marcel Duchamp's uproar-igniting *Fountain*, his most famous ready-made work. This glazed ceramic urinal is a replica Duchamp created in 1964; the 1917 original was lost. The fine photography collection includes works by Alfred Stieglitz, Edward Weston, Ansel Adams, Dorothea Lange, Robert Frank, and William Klein.

The museum is currently being expanded to accommodate the Fisher Collection, which includes works by Alexander Calder, Chuck Close, Roy Lichtenstein, and Andy Warhol.

YERBA BUENA GARDENS

Cross Third Street into the lovely **Yerba Buena Gardens** ❺ (www.yerbabuena gardens.com; Mon–Sun 6am–10pm;

SFMOMA   *Museum of the African Diaspora*

free). Yerba Buena was the name of the first European settlement in the area. In 1835 an English sailor named William Richardson set up a trading post called "Yerba Buena," named after the wild mint ("good herb" in Spanish) that grew locally. Six months after the sleepy settlement was claimed for the U.S. in 1846, it was renamed San Francisco.

Today, the gardens are a two-square-block urban oasis featuring grassy landscaping, public artwork, and an old-fashioned merry-go-round popular with children. There is also a waterfall memorial dedicated to Dr. Martin Luther King, Jr.

On the southwest corner is the Metreon (www.westfield.com/metreon) an entertainment complex with some 15

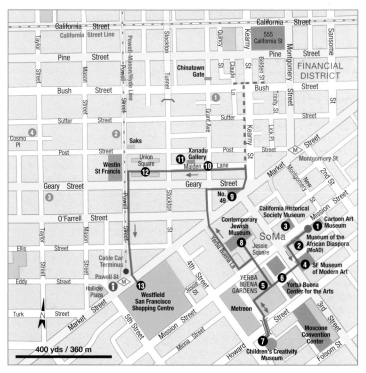

Martin Luther King Jr. memorial

theaters, a giant Imax screen, shops, and restaurants, which really comes into its own on rainy days.

Located in a two-building complex, the **Yerba Buena Center for the Arts** ❻ (YBCA, 701 Mission Street; tel: 978-2787; www.ybca.org; gallery hours: Tue–Sat noon–8pm, Sun noon–6pm; charge except 1st Tue of month) exhibits contemporary art along with community-based work and also presents contemporary dance, theater, music, and cross-disciplinary performances from both national and international performers.

One block south, and very much geared towards children, is the **Children's Creativity Museum** ❼ (221 Fourth Street; tel: 820-3320; http://creativity.org; Wed–Sun noon–4pm; charge).

Among the attractions here are an ice-skating rink, bowling center, and carrousel (daily 11am–6pm), as well as the museum itself: a hands-on multimedia arts and technology museum that teaches children about animation, digital technology, and electronic media and helps them create movies, music, and art.

Next to the Children's Creativity Museum is the largest structure in the heart of SoMa: the **Moscone Convention Center**, which hosts most of the major conventions held in the city each month. On top of the center is one of the largest city-owned solar installations in the country.

SOCIETY OF CALIFORNIA PIONEERS MUSEUM

Exit Yerba Buena onto Mission Street to reach the **Contemporary Jewish Museum** ❽ (736 Mission Street; www.thecjm.org; Mon–Tue, Thur–Sun 11am–5pm, Thur 11am–8pm; charge), which focuses on Jewish art and culture. The facility designed by architect Daniel Libeskind – also responsible for New York City's Freedom Tower – incorporates the historic Jessie Street Power Substation. Exit the museum and turn right to find the charming pedestrian Yerba Buena Lane, a quiet enclave of stores and restaurants.

49 GEARY STREET

Exit Yerba Buena Lane onto Market Street and cross onto Grant Avenue. Then turn right on Geary Street to reach the high-rise at **49 Geary Street** ❾, a particularly popular art gallery address that houses the renowned Fraenkel Gallery among others. The cluster of galleries around Union Square is the city's thickest (several more galleries are found on nearby Sutter Street). For a handy guide of maps, addresses, and details on specific events, refer to www.sfbayareagalleryguide.com.

On the first Tuesday of the month, many museums offer free admission. On the first Thursday of each month, the San Francisco tradition of "First Thursdays" turns typically calm galleries into

Merry-go-round   *Maiden Lane*

lively, wine-sipping social events. Many galleries schedule their show openings and then keep their door open later than usual.

MAIDEN LANE

Now turn left off Geary onto Kearny Street. For an alfresco lunch or dinner detour, head to north to Bush Street. Turn right to find the European-inspired Belden Place, or for the French-focused Claude Alley. At both you can enjoy bistro fare, and a casual, romantic ambience with outside seating. The little-known French Quarter is particularly lively each year on Bastille Day (July 14).

Otherwise, turn left from Geary on **Maiden Lane ❿**. Maiden Lane's tongue-in-cheek name originated from its notorious red-light past during the city's rowdy "Barbary Coast" days. Then the lane was called Morton Street and was known for having the cheapest prostitutes in town. When the brothels burned down in the 1906 fire, Maiden Lane rose from the ashes.

Today the two cool, shaded blocks conduct anything but shady business: they are studded with glossy boutiques such as **Chanel** and candelier **Diptyche**, along with seamstress seventh heaven **Britex Fabrics** and San Francisco institution Gump's. Gump's started years ago by selling frames and mirrors to bars and bordellos during the Gold-Rush era, then moved upscale to the present-day store, which is more

akin to a museum selling the best in jade, glassware, silks, and antiques.

At No. 140 is the **Xanadu Gallery ⓫** (www.folkartintl.com; Tue–Sat 10am–6pm; free), a collection of artwork, textiles, jewelry, and artifacts from around the world that is located in the city's only building designed by architect Frank Lloyd Wright.

UNION SQUARE

At the end of Maiden Lane, cross Stockton Street into **Union Square ⓬**, where the city's shopping pulse thumps most wildly. The streets are stacked with international luxury retailers such as **Cartier** and **Hermès**, and elegant emporia including **Saks Fifth Avenue**, **Macy's**, and **Neiman Marcus**. The latter is crowned by an exquisite stained-glass rotunda salvaged from the City of Paris, San Francisco's first department store and the site's original occupant.

Union Square provides a place of repose for the weary shopper. The square is as old as San Francisco itself. First deeded for public use in 1850, it got its name a decade later when it was used to rally support for the Union cause during the Civil War. At the square's center is a 90ft (27m) Corinthian column topped by a bronze Victory commemorating the successful Manila Bay campaign during the Spanish-American War of 1898.

To have a break from shopping, stop for French bistro fare at **Café de la Presse ❶**, a hearty meal at **Sears Fine Food ❷**,

The Zeum complex

cocktails at the **Redwood Room** ③, or wine at **The Barrel Room** ④.

WESTFIELD SAN FRANCISCO SHOPPING CENTRE

From Union Square, head south on Powell to Market Street, past the cable-car terminus of the Powell–Hyde and Powell–Mason routes. The stairway on the right descends to the **San Francisco Visitor Center** (www.sanfrancisco.travel), which provides useful information in 14 languages on dining, accommodation, tours, and transportation for the city and nearby destinations. Cross Market Street for the **Westfield San Francisco Shopping Centre** ⑬ (865 Market Street; http://westfield.com; Mon–Sat 9.30am–9pm, Sun 10am–7pm), an indoor mall with unusual escalators that spiral around a nine-story atrium, whisking shoppers to **Nordstrom** at the top. There is also an upmarket **Bloomingdales** and a large downstairs food court.

Food and Drink

① CAFÉ DE LA PRESSE

352 Grant Avenue; tel: 398-2680; www.cafedelapresse.com; daily B, L, and D; $$

Join the European literati at the tables that spill out onto the sidewalk at this charming French café. Dine on sandwiches, Alsatian tarts, and other classic French bistro fare, washed down with espresso shots and glasses of beer and wine. Inside, international magazines and newspapers are sold.

② SEARS FINE FOOD

439 Powell Street; tel: 986-0700; daily B, L, and D; $$

The Swedish pancakes are legendary here, but this dependable diner also boasts an extended and tasty menu for brunch (until 3pm each day) and beyond.

③ REDWOOD ROOM AT THE CLIFT HOTEL

495 Geary Street; tel: 982-6168; www.clifthotel.com; Sun–Thur 5pm–2am, Fri–Sat 4pm–2am; drinks only

Redesigned by Philippe Starck, this historic San Francisco hotel bar retains its elegance, but with a modern twist (note how the eyes of the paintings move). The handsome redwood bar was carved from a single tree.

④ THE BARREL ROOM

1/2 Cosmo Place (off Taylor); tel: 674-3567; www.thehiddenvine.com; Tue–Thur 5pm–midnight; Fri–Sat 5pm–2am; $$

After a busy day walking and shopping around Union Square, sink into a comfy armchair in this cozy, den-like wine bar and relax with a glass of small-production, terroir-expressive wine and a cheese plate or flatbread.

San Francisco Public Library

CIVIC CENTER AND
HAYES VALLEY

*The grand government and cultural buildings of San Francisco's Civic Center
are sandwiched by the Tenderloin – one of the city's poorest areas – and the smart
Hayes Valley, with its upscale boutiques, restaurants, galleries, and bars.*

DISTANCE: 1 mile (2km)
TIME: 2–3 hours (this includes a visit
to the Asian Art Museum)
START: San Francisco Public Library
END: Hayes Street
POINTS TO NOTE: Because neighborhoods just outside the area covered by
this tour can be unsafe, it is best not to
wander off the path: the Tenderloin area
to the north is as gritty as it gets. The
tour begins at the San Francisco Public
Library (BART: Civic Center station; bus:
5, 6, 7, 19, 21, 47, 49, 71 F).

Compact Civic Center is awash with
civic life and underpinned by city government, cultural institutions, and a
cluster of visual and expressive arts
venues. Arthur Brown, Jr (1874–1957),
the most celebrated architect of his era,
was responsible for many of the Beaux
Arts structures. While Civic Center's
rebirth happened in the early 20th century, it's only in the last 20 years that
Hayes Valley has undergone its biggest
transformation, from an urban no-go

area to one full of diverse restaurants
and some of the hippest shops in town.

SAN FRANCISCO PUBLIC
LIBRARY, MAIN BRANCH

The imposing main branch of the Beaux
Arts **San Francisco Public Library** ❶
(100 Larkin Street; http://sfpl.org; Mon
10am–6pm, Tue–Thur 9am–8pm, Fri
noon–6pm, Sat 10am–6pm, Sun noon–
5pm) opened on April 18, 1996. Visitors
are greeted by a stately white granite
facade, and inside, a lofty central atrium
basks in natural light pouring in from
a dramatic skylight. Behind the public library's grand staircase is Nayland
Blake's five-story *Constellation* (1996),
an artwork that uses fiber-optic beams
to illuminate inscriptions of 160 writers'
names on glass shades.

Visit the third floor for the American Center, the Chinese Center, and the
James C. Hormel Gay & Lesbian Center.
The last was the first resource center of
its kind in a public institution, with books,
photographs, films, and memorabilia
documenting LGBT history and culture.

Asian Art Museum

Higher floors are home to music and environmental centers, which offer resources and exhibits related to those subjects.

ASIAN ART MUSEUM

North of the library is the impressive **Asian Art Museum** ❷ (200 Larkin Street; www.asianart.org; Tue–Sun 10am–5pm, Thur until 9pm; charge, 1st Sun of month free). In 2003, after decades in Golden Gate Park, the museum moved to this Beaux Arts building that had been redesigned by Gae Aulenti. The structure formerly hosted the main library; now instead of books, it has paintings, sculptures, ceramics, stoneware, basketry, puppets, weaponry, and textiles. With 18,000 artworks spanning 6,000 years of history, this is one of the world's most comprehensive collections of Asian art.

The collection

Special rotating exhibits are shown on the first floor, while the second and third floors showcase around 2,000 pieces from the permanent collection in regionally grouped galleries that cover China, Japan, Korea, India, Iran, the Himalayas, and Southeast Asia.

Among the many highlights are Chinese jades and ceramics; Japanese bamboo baskets (the largest collection outside of Japan) and rare painted scrolls; Korean celadons and textiles; a Burmese 19th-century crowned and enthroned Buddha; Thai paintings; Indonesian puppets; Southeast Asian *krises* (daggers); Indian Buddhist stone sculptures; and Sikh art. One not-to-be-missed treasure is a gilded bronze Buddha on the third floor, inscribed AD 338; it is the oldest dated Chinese Buddha known in world. It is also one of some 7,700 objects donated by

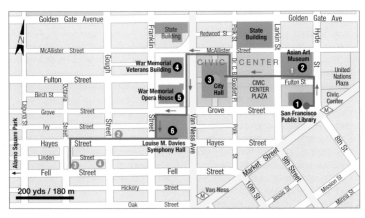

Detail of a gate at City Hall   The grand interior of City Hall

Avery Brundage, the Chicago industrialist whose endowment in the 1960s sparked the museum's creation. After your tour of the collections, you might want to stop off at the **Café Asia** ➊, to refuel.

SAN FRANCISCO CITY HALL

Walk across the tree- and flag-lined walkways of Civic Center Plaza past lawns and sculptures to San Francisco's **City Hall** ➌ (1 Dr. Carlton B. Goodlett Place; www.sfgov.org; Mon–Fri 8am–8pm; free). Built in 1914 and occupying two spacious city blocks, the building was influenced by the City Beautiful movement of the 1890s and is perhaps the grandest seat of city government in the U.S., representing the city's optimism at the end of the century. The splendid 306ft (93m) bronze-and-gold-leaf dome that dominates the skyline is the fifth-largest in the world, dwarfing the U.S. Capitol Building in Washington D.C. by some 42in (107cm). San Francisco-based architect Arthur Brown, Jr. (1874–1957) designed the structure, including the finishing details such as doorknobs and floor patterns.

Inside, an airy and open rotunda with white limestone walls and a floor of Tennessee pink marble serves as a backdrop for post-nuptial photo opportunities on the sweeping staircase. Back in 1954, City Hall witnessed the marriage of Joe DiMaggio and Marilyn Monroe. Flanking the rotunda are the North and South Light Courts; the latter is home to exhibits, art-

works, and a clock with a design unique to City Hall, with the Roman numeral IV spelled (deliberately) as IIII.

City Hall was the scene of the murders of Harvey Milk and Mayor George Moscone in 1978, and in February 2004 it found itself at the center of nationwide controversy when Mayor Gavin Newsom granted marriage licenses to same-sex couples; around 4,000 flocked to City Hall to exchange their vows before the California Supreme Court shut down the proceedings.

Hayes Boutiques

Hayes Street between Franklin and Laguna streets is a fun place to boutique-hop. For fashion, try **Azalea** (411 Hayes Street, www.azaleasf.com) for clothes and accessories, **Ver Unica** (437B Hayes Street, www.verunicasf.com) for quality vintage, and **Outer Layer** (498 Hayes Street; www.marinelayer.com) for locally made, comfortable basics. Home design all-stars include **Maker & Moss** (364 Hayes Street, www.makerandmoss.com) for a mix of high-low artisanal wares. And then there are the specialty stores. **Flight 001** (525 Hayes Street; www.flight 001.com) supplies mod jet-setting gear, and **Nancy Boy** (347 Hayes Street; www.nancyboy.com) markets high-end body products. **True Sake** (560 Hayes, www.truesake.com) boasts over 220 bottles of Japanese rice wine! Most stores open from 10–11am to 6–7pm.

The War Memorial Veterans Building

The War Memorial Opera House has also witnessed important diplomatic events. It was on the Opera House stage on June 26, 1945 that President Truman signed the United Nations charter, and the building also saw the signing of the San Francisco Peace Treaty between the United States and Japan, which officially ended hostilities between the two world powers in 1951.

Sign up at the Docent Tour kiosk by the elevators in the Van Ness Avenue lobby for a 45-minute tour (tel: 554-6139; Mon–Fri 10am, noon and 2pm; free except for groups of eight or more).

WAR MEMORIAL VETERANS BUILDING

From City Hall walk north on Dr Carlton B. Goodlett Place and turn left on McAllister Street. Then turn left on Van Ness Avenue to reach the **War Memorial Veterans Building** ❹ at No. 401, one of a pair of nearly identical Beaux Arts buildings that comprise the War Memorial Complex. The Veterans Building is home to the 916-seat **Herbst Theater** as well as the **San Francisco Arts Commission Gallery** (www.sfartscommission.org/gallery.org; Wed–Sat noon–5pm; free), with its diverse contemporary art exhibits.

WAR MEMORIAL OPERA HOUSE

Continue walking south on Van Ness Avenue, reaching the **War Memorial Opera House** ❺ at No. 301. The building features a long, marble-floored foyer, a vaulted and coffered ceiling, and a handsome 3,146-seat hall, through which the first aria soared on October 15, 1932, to the tune of Giacomo Puccini's *Tosca*.

The **San Francisco Opera** (tel: 861-4008, box office 864-3330; www.sfopera.com) performs here September–November and May–July. During its off-season, the **San Francisco Ballet** (tel: 865-2000; www.sfballet.org) takes the stage, presenting traditional ballets and modern dance, and a very popular *Nutcracker* production each December.

LOUISE M. DAVIES SYMPHONY HALL

Just across Grove Street, the elegant **Louise M. Davies Symphony Hall** ❻ (201 Van Ness Avenue) houses the **San Francisco Symphony Orchestra** (tel: 864-6000; www.sfsymphony.org), whose main season runs September–July. Tours are offered of Louise M. Davies Symphony Hall, the War Memorial Opera House, and Herbst Theatre (tel: 552-8338; Mon 10am–2pm, on the hour; charge). Meet at the Grove Street entrance of Louise M. Davies Symphony Hall. From Van Ness, turn right on Grove Street, left on Franklin Street, and right on Hayes Street.

HAYES VALLEY

After the 1989 earthquake rendered unsafe a portion of the Central Freeway that hovered menacingly over Hayes

War Memorial Opera House

Café mural, Hayes Valley

Valley, a large chunk of it was removed and the once drug- and prostitute-riddled neighborhood shifted suddenly into a hip retail center with art galleries, fashion boutiques, specialty stores selling everything from sake to travel accessories, and a bevy of restaurants serving up German schnitzel, Mediterranean kebabs, Chicago pizza, French bistro fare, and more.

To soak up the Hayes Valley shopping scene, walk west on Hayes Street toward Laguna Street. For a quick bite or coffee stop **Arlequin To Go ❷**, or walk a few blocks more for German beer, soft pretzels, and bratwurst at **Biergar-**

ten ❸. If caffeine is all you crave, turn left onto Octavia Street, walk along the community park, and then turn left onto Linden Street for the **Blue Bottle Coffee Company ❹**.

The Painted Ladies

If you're still not tired, walk west (or catch the 21 bus) up Hayes Street another four blocks to Alamo Square Park. This hillside park offers a view not only of the downtown skyscrapers and Civic Center, but also of the famous "Painted Ladies," a picturesque row of colorful and ornate Victorian homes nicknamed "postcard row."

Food and Drink

❶ CAFÉ ASIA

Asian Art Museum, 200 Larkin Street; tel: 581-3630; www.asianart.org/cafeasia.htm; Tue–Sun 10am–4.30pm (Thur to 8.30pm); $

Café Asia is a casual, convenient spot for refueling after touring the vast collections, with cafeteria-style service, indoor and outdoor seating, and plenty of Pan-Asian fare and café standards.

❷ ARLEQUIN TO GO

384 Hayes Street; tel: 626-1211; www.arlequincafe.com; Mon 8am–7pm, Tue–Fri 8am–8pm, Sat 9am–8pm, Sun 9am–7pm; $

Do not let the name fool you: this small café opens up to a wide, lush garden in the back,

and is a great place to enjoy top-quality café food with an espresso or a glass of beer or wine.

❸ BIERGARTEN

424 Octavia St; www.biergartensf.com; Wed–Sat 2–8pm, Sun 1–7pm, $$

An offshoot from the German restaurant Suppenküche across the street, this beer garden serves up liter mugs of German beer, along with traditional soft pretzels, *bratwurst*, and deviled eggs.

❹ BLUE BOTTLE COFFEE COMPANY

315 Linden Street; www.bluebottlecoffee.com; Mon–Fri 7am–6pm, Sat–Sun 8am–6pm; $

This popular, tiny to-go kiosk serves espressos, drip coffee, New Orleans iced coffee, cookies and *biscotti*.

View of Bay Bridge from Nob Hill

NOB HILL AND RUSSIAN HILL

Soak up Nob Hill's old-fashioned refinement with its grand hotels and the Gothic Grace Cathedral and then explore tony Russian Hill's hidden stairways, crooked streets, and charming cafés, restaurants, and boutiques.

DISTANCE: 2.5 miles (4km)
TIME: A half-day
START: Inter-Continental Mark Hopkins San Francisco
END: Polk Street
POINTS TO NOTE: This tour's several very steep hills and stairways make it unsuitable for wheelchair-users. To reach the starting point, bus: 1 to Mason Street; cable-car: Powell–Hyde or Powell–Mason line to California Street, or California line to Mason Street.

This tour begins on the crest of stately Nob Hill, at California and Mason streets. With its imposing hotels and breathtaking vistas, Nob Hill exudes grandeur and good breeding, offering a glimpse of the pomp and decadence of the early days of San Francisco. Formerly known as California Hill, Nob Hill was originally just steeply sloped scrubland. With the advent of the cable-car, however, its peak became easily accessible and allowed the city's elite to turn it into an exclusive neighborhood of palatial mansions and fine restaurants some 376ft (115m) above the city.

EXCLUSIVE ENCLAVE

Nob Hill has always had a reputation for being home to privilege and luxury. Some believe the word "Nob" was derived from "nabob," a British term for the rich that was derived from the Indian word for Moghul prince; others say Nob is simply a version of "knob," meaning a rounded hill.

This was where the "Big Four" of the Central Pacific Railroad – Leland Stanford, Charles Crocker, Mark Hopkins, and Collis Huntington – built opulent estates, only to see them demolished by the 1906 earthquake and fire. From the ashes of their mansions rose world-famous luxury hotels, continuing the neighborhood's tradition of privilege.

Inter-Continental Mark Hopkins

The southeast corner of California and Mason streets hosts the towering **Inter-Continental Mark Hopkins San Francisco ❶** (1 Nob Hill; tel: 392-3434; www.

intercontinentalmarkhopkins.com), on the former site of railway tycoon Mark Hopkins's mansion. The home had lavish stables with rosewood stalls, silver trimmings, and mosaic floors covered with Belgian carpets. Hopkins saw much of this luxury destroyed in the fire that raged for three days and nights following the earthquake of 1906, but the house was soon rebuilt. The hotel opened to great fanfare in 1926 and bespeaks sky-high class, all the way up to the 19th-floor **Top of the Mark bar** and its tall crow's nest, where the largest U.S. flag flying in San Francisco proudly flaps.

Renaissance Stanford Court

Look east to 905 California for the **Renaissance Stanford Court Hotel ②** (tel: 989-3500; www.stanfordcourt.com). Another result of the 1906 destruction, this hotel was built in 1911 in the place of the ruined mansion of Leland Stanford, who lent his name to the university he founded with his wife in Palo Alto, California.

The Fairmont San Francisco

Walk north on Mason Street past the regal-looking **Fairmont San Francisco ③** (950 Mason Street; tel: 772-5000;

Nob Hill Spa

www.fairmont.com/san-francisco), a hotel that once dominated the San Francisco skyline, and where Tony Bennett first sang *I Left My Heart in San Francisco*.

Built by Tessie and Virginia Fair as a lavish testament to their father James "Bonanza Jim" Graham Fair (once one of the richest men in San Francisco), the hotel was completed just before the 1906 disaster only to have the sumptuous interiors ruined by the fire. It was speedily rebuilt, with the remodeling overseen by Julia Morgan, and re-opened triumphantly just a year to the day after the devastating event.

PACIFIC-UNION CLUB

The brownstone across Mason Street from the Fairmont was the only neighborhood estate left standing after the 1906 disaster. Built by silver magnate James Cair Flood, the Connecticut sandstone building, designed by Willis Polk, is considered the first of its kind to be constructed west of the Mississippi. It's now home to the private, prestigious, and men-only **Pacific-Union Club ❹**.

BROCKLEBANK BUILDING

Walk north on Mason to the corner of Mason and Sacramento streets to enjoy fine vistas to the north and east. This brings you to the **Brocklebank Building ❺**, former home of legendary *San Francisco Chronicle* columnist Herb Caen. The building may look familiar to enthusiasts of film director Alfred Hitchcock: along with a flashy forest-green Jaguar parked out front, it featured in his San Francisco-set film classic, *Vertigo* (1958).

HUNTINGTON PARK

Walk west on Sacramento to reach the genteel greenery of bench-lined **Huntington Park ❻**. Once the site of railroad lawyer David Colton's mansion, this is a lovely place to lounge, browse an occasional weekend art show, enjoy the view of neighboring Grace Cathedral, and do some people-watching. The central fountain is a replica of the Tartarughe Fountain in Rome's Piazza Mattei. Across California Street is the Huntington Hotel, which began life in the 1920s as the 140-room Huntington Apartments. Today, the Huntington's Big 4 restaurant celebrates Crocker, Hopkins, Huntington, and Stanford, and evokes the robber baron era with its woody, masculine interior. The hotel is also home to the luxurious Nob Hill Spa (www.nobhillspa. com). One building down is the Masonic Center. Commissioned by the California Freemasons after the end of World War II, it is now an event center hosting cultural performances.

GRACE CATHEDRAL

Across Taylor Street from Huntington Park, climb the cascade of white steps to stately **Grace Cathedral ❼**

Cable-car winding wheels   *Gates of Paradise, Grace Cathedral*

(1100 California Street; www.gracecathedral.org; Sun–Fri 7am–6pm, Sat 8am–6pm; donation appreciated), which sits on land gifted by the Charles Crocker family.

Finished in 1964, the cathedral is an Episcopal tribute to the French Gothic style. Outside the east entrance are casts of Lorenzo Ghiberti's 15th-century, 16ft (5m) -high, bronze-and-gold doors, called the **Gates of Paradise**. Originally sculpted for the Baptistery of the cathedral in Florence, they depict stories from the Old and New testaments.

The interior

Inside the cathedral, colorful paintings decorate the walls, and light streams through stained glass of rich blues, reds, and yellows. Charles Connick's **23rd Psalm Window** above the southern entrance echoes Chartres Cathedral's Jesse Window, while Gabriel Loire's **Rose Window** above the east entrance depicts St. Francis's poem *The Canticle of the Sun*. A small recess houses the **Aids Interfaith Chapel**, which is dedicated to those affected by Aids. The chapel features an altarpiece by Keith Haring as well as a colorful panel from the Aids Memorial Quilt (www.aids quilt.org), a project begun in 1987 when the devastating epidemic was ravaging San Francisco. The cathedral also features two labyrinths, one made of terrazzo in a courtyard outside the church, and another made of limestone inside.

CABLE-CAR MUSEUM

Exit the church and turn left onto the quietly picturesque Taylor Street. If you are hungry, nab a sidewalk table at **Nob Hill Café** ❶. Turn right at Washington and teeter down towards the red brick **Cable-Car Museum** ❽ (1201 Mason Street; daily 10am–5pm, Apr–Sept to 6pm; free). Built in 1910, this historic cable-car barn and powerhouse displays antique cable-cars, engines, winding wheels, and other mechanical devices that help the beloved moving National Monuments run smoothly. Just how do they work? The cars are pulled by a wire cable that runs beneath the street; the gripman uses a clamp located beneath the carriage to hold or release the cable, which pulls the cable car along the street. San Francisco's cable cars are now among the last in the United States, with at least 100 cities having abandoned them for buses.

INA COOLBRITH PARK

Walk north on Mason Street. At Vallejo Street turn left to reach the stairways marking the entrance of the **Ina Coolbrith Park** ❾. Coolbrith was an Oakland librarian and California's first poet laureate; she also mentored a young Jack London and entertained other literary greats at her home on nearby Macondray Lane. These steep stairways climb to small, narrow lookout ledges peppered with pine trees, cacti, and green benches. Though a challenging climb, it offers dra-

Snaking Lombard Street

matic, sweeping panoramas of North Beach, Telegraph Hill, and Coit Tower, the length of Bay Bridge, the TransAmerica building, and downtown San Francisco. Now you have reached the breezy top of upscale Russian Hill, named for the Russians buried in a cemetery here in the early days of San Francisco.

FEUSIER HOUSE AND 1907 FIREHOUSE

When you emerge from the park you will be on Vallejo Street; walk down to Jones Street and turn right. Then turn left at Green Street to reach the **Feusier House** ⓾, an eight-sided oddity built in 1857 when octagonal houses were thought to be economical and healthy due to increased sunlight and better ventilation. Across the street at 1088 Green Street is the old 1907 **Firehouse** ⓫, bought from the city in 1957 by Louise M. Davies, for whom the city's symphony hall is named. Both houses are private residences and closed to the public. Return to Jones Street and turn left, descending the steps on the east side. On Jones between Green and Union streets, sneak a peek down **Macondray Lane** ⓬, a beautifully woodsy and secluded lane with a secret-garden ambience. Overgrown and lined with paths of uneven brick and stone, it is the real-life counterpart to Barbary Lane in Armistead Maupin's *Tales of the City*, a series that chronicled life in San Francisco from the mid-1970s to the mid-1980s. Turn left at Chestnut Street.

SAN FRANCISCO ART INSTITUTE

At 800 Chestnut Street stands the **San Francisco Art Institute** ⓭ (www.sfai. edu; Tue–Sat 11am–6pm; free), an educational establishment founded in 1871, which also hosts temporary exhibits open to the public. Located in a gorgeous 1920s Spanish Revival building, the school was responsible for the education of American talents like Annie Leibovitz, Mark Rothko, Ansel Adams, and Dorothea Lange. Pass through the courtyard

Cable-Car Central

San Francisco's Cable-Car Museum is the nerve center of the transportation system invented by London-born American immigrant Andrew Smith Hallidie (1836–1900), that was once ridiculed as "Hallidie's Folly," because no one thought it would actually work. Here, electric motors drive the huge winding machinery, which keep the cables running through slots in the street at a constant speed of 9.5mph (15kph). Today there are 40 cable-cars in the city's system, with a maximum of 26 running along the three lines at any given time. It may seem impressive that a cable-car can take you all the way from Market and Powell streets to Fisherman's Wharf, but the 5 miles (8km) of track in use is nothing compared to the 75 miles (121km) along which the eight original companies' cable-cars used to creak.

Nob Hill at sunset

to the gallery on the left, which houses the institute's most important permanent work of art, *Making of a Fresco Showing the Building of a City* (1931) by Mexican artist Diego Rivera. The fresco within a fresco features Rivera on a scaffold surrounded by others who worked on the artwork. Step onto the fresh breeze-swept terraces to enjoy a bite at the café and soak up views of the bay, North Beach, Coit Tower, and Russian Hill.

LOMBARD STREET

Continue up Chestnut Street and turn left at Leavenworth Street. Pass the twin gazebos and rose bushes of dime-sized **Fay Park** ⑭ on the left (Wed–Thur and Sun 10am–4pm). This historic Thomas Church garden was designed in 1957 and bequeathed to the city in 1998. Turn right up the famously twisty **Lombard Street** ⑮, a one-way block with eight hairpin turns known as the "crookedest street in the world" (although San Francisco's own Vermont Avenue at 20th Street is actually more bendy). Although tales vary, one theory for the curves is that they were carved in the 1920s in order to allow horses to negotiate the hill. Climb Lombard, admiring the flowery landscaping and ivy-covered private residences.

HYDE AND POLK STREETS

Turn left onto leafy Hyde Street, lined with clusters of cafés, elegant bistros, and antique stores, and traversed by the whirring Powell–Hyde cable-car. As you pass Filbert Street, note the sudden drop-off on the left after half a block; the 31.5 percent gradient descent is the city's steepest. At Hyde and Union, order an ice cream at **Swensen's** ②, a city institution. Turn right on Green Street and end the tour with dinner in the Russian Hill hub of **Polk Street**, which is packed with restaurants, popular bars, cafés, and shops.

The Peace Plaza

JAPANTOWN, PACIFIC HEIGHTS, AND COW HOLLOW

Wander from Japantown through affluent Pacific Heights and its neighbor Cow Hollow, taking in the handsome architecture of private mansions and townhouses, hilltop parks with dramatic views, and chic cafés, restaurants, and boutiques.

DISTANCE: 3 miles (5km)
TIME: A half-day
START: Japan Center
END: Union and Gough streets
POINTS TO NOTE: The Haas-Lilienthal House tour is only offered Wed, Sat, or Sun afternoons. Unless otherwise noted, the residences mentioned are closed to the public, and the privacy of the owners should be respected. This tour begins at the Japan Center (bus: 1, 12, 22, 24).

Largely residential, the three central neighborhoods of Japantown, Pacific Heights, and Cow Hollow all have their own thriving commercial centers and boast some of the best examples of San Francisco architecture. Fillmore Street is a major north–south route that links the three.

JAPANTOWN

Compact Japantown is a cultural hub for the city's Japanese community and is dominated by the **Japan Center** ❶ (Post Street, between Fillmore and Laguna streets; www.sfjapantown. org). This 5-acre (2-hectare) complex of Japanese restaurants and boutiques designed by Minoru Yamasaki is filled with elegant home decor, vintage silk kimonos, and Japanese-language books. The **Peace Plaza** is home to the 100ft (30m) Peace Pagoda designed by Yoshiro Taniguchi and presented in friendship to the people of the U.S. from the people of Japan after World War II.

World War II was a tumultuous time for Japanese Americans living in San Francisco. At least 110,000 *Nisei* (second-generation Japanese) had their property seized, and were rounded up and sent to detention camps in the xenophobic days after Pearl Harbor. Accused of no crime, they lived behind barbed wire under military guard. Americans of Japanese heritage were estimated to have lost $365 million in property from having to sell their homes at under-market prices at this time. It wasn't until 1988, after a pro-

Japantown sculpture   *View from Alta Plaza Park*

longed battle, that $1.6 billion in reparations was set aside by the federal government for surviving internees and their heirs.

Exit onto Post Street and turn left, passing the **Sundance Kabuki** ❷ (1881 Post Street; tel: 929-4650; www.sundancecinemas.com). This upscale, remodeled theater presents independent films and blockbusters, as well as much of the San Francisco International Film Festival, held every spring. Unlike most movie theaters, here you can reserve specific seats, as well as bring alcoholic beverages and food into certain 21+ showings.

FILLMORE STREET

Continue along Post Street and turn right at Fillmore Street, the place to enjoy the luxury of Pacific Heights. Among Fillmore Street's stylish offerings are international fashion-forward footwear at Gimme Shoes (No. 2358; www.gimmeshoes.com; Mon–Sat 11am–7pm, Sun noon–6pm) and whimsical, Parisian-style home goods at Nest (No. 2300; tel: 292-6199; www.nestsf.com; Mon–Fri 10.30am–6.30pm, Sat 10.30am–6pm, Sun 11am–6pm).

Pick up some French pastries at **La Boulange** ❶, or for a more substantial start on weekends, try brunch at **Elite Café** ❷.

Continue north to find the **Clay Theatre** ❸ (2261 Fillmore Street; tel: 267-4893; www.landmarktheatres.com).

Of the dying, single-screen breed, this comfy one-time nickelodeon built in 1910 now hosts independent films and popular midnight screenings of classics.

ALTA PLAZA PARK

From Fillmore Street, detour left on Washington Street to reach **Alta Plaza Park** ❹, designed by the legendary Golden Gate Park landscaper John McLaren. Staggered stairways climb grassy terraces to reach basketball and tennis courts, and sweeping city views.

Swanky Spas

The Pacific Heights area is home to several of San Francisco's plush pampering options. In Japantown, **Kabuki Springs and Spa** (1750 Geary Boulevard; tel: 922-6000; www.kabukisprings.com; daily 10am–9.45pm) is a serene setting for facials, acupuncture, massages, and traditional communal baths. Named for the eye-popping paint hue used on the Golden Gate Bridge, **International Orange** (2nd floor, 2044 Fillmore Street; tel: 630-5928; www.internationalorange.com; Mon–Fri 9am–9pm, Sat–Sun 9am–8pm) is a fresh-feeling day spa with a relaxing redwood sundeck. It offers yoga classes and treatments such as massages, facials, and acupuncture.

Hilly Pacific Heights

LAFAYETTE PARK

For even more views, backtrack along Washington Street to cross Fillmore Street and continue on to **Lafayette Park ❺**. Here, you can take in the beautiful panoramas from a four-block swathe of greenery that is dusted with pinecones and eucalyptus leaves, and surrounded by stately Pacific Heights mansions.

SPRECKELS MANSION

On the north side of Lafayette Park, sneak a peek north at the grand Beaux-Arts **Spreckels Mansion ❻** (2080 Washington Street), partially obscured by tall shrubbery. Built in 1913 for Alma de Bretteville Spreckels and her sugar-heir husband Adolph Spreckels (the same Spreckels that donated the Palace of the Legion of Honor Art Museum to the City of San Francisco in 1924), the imposing white limestone contains 55 rooms, including a Louis XVI-style ballroom. The gate on the

Jackson Street side was the old delivery entrance, and behind the window in the wall was where the gatekeeper lived. Now the residence is owned by the best-selling romantic novelist Danielle Steele.

Local jazz festival   *The Haas–Lilienthal House*

HAAS-LILIENTHAL HOUSE

Continue east on Washington Street and turn north on Franklin Street to tour the **Haas-Lilienthal House** ❼ (No. 2007; tel: 441-3004; www. sfheritage.org; tours Wed and Sat noon–3pm, Sun 11am–4pm; call in advance on Sat as is sometimes closed for private functions; charge). This Queen Anne-style Victorian mansion with elaborate wooden gables was designed by Bavarian architect Peter Schmidt and built in 1886. It is the city's only intact Victorian from the period to be regularly open as a museum, complete with original furniture and artifacts, and was occupied by the same family until 1972.

WHITTIER MANSION

Continuing on Franklin, turn left onto Jackson Street to reach the **Whittier Mansion** ❽ (No. 2090), built in 1896 for William Frank Whittier, a prominent businessman. Designed by Edward R. Swain, the building survived the 1906 earthquake thanks to its construction of stone on a steel framework, then a state-of-the-art technique in San Francisco. Over the years, people have reported ghostly sightings or a ghostly presence in the basement of the Whittier Mansion. Most believe it is the ghost of Whittier himself, who died in 1917, but others suggest it is his ne'er-do-well son Billy, who when

alive, used to frequent the servants' quarters and his father's wine cellar for "wine, women, and song."

JAMES LEARY FLOOD MANSION

At this point in the route, continue on Franklin and turn right on Buchanan Street and left on Broadway Street to reach the school quarters and administrative buildings of the **Society of the Sacred Heart**. The **Grant House** ❾ (No. 2220) and its exquisite neighbor, the three-story **James Leary Flood Mansion** ❿ (No. 2222; www. floodmansion.org) form part of the complex.

Designed in 1912 by Bliss and Faville and completed in time for the 1915 Panama-Pacific World Exposition, the former Flood residence is a stunning combination of architecture styles. A courtyard on the north side of the house offers a dazzling view of the bay, while the interiors are beautifully dressed in marble, hand-carved woods, and hand-painted murals.

3119 FILLMORE STREET

From Broadway, turn right on Fillmore Street for a steep descent to Union Street. On October 13, 1955, Allen Ginsberg first performed his legendary poem *Howl*, at the now-defunct Gallery Six that used to occupy 3119 Fillmore Street. Ginsberg ended the reading in tears, the audience went

Old Vedanta Society Temple

wild, and Ginsberg's friend and fellow Beatnik Jack Kerouac declared, "Ginsberg, this poem will make you famous in San Francisco." Kerouac memorialized the epic night in his 1958 novel *Dharma Bums* when one of the characters recites the poem *Wail*.

Steep streets in Pacific Heights

OLD VEDANTA SOCIETY TEMPLE

Turn right on Union Street and left on Webster Street to reach the turreted, lavender-hued **Old Vedanta Society Temple ⑪** (No. 2963; www.sfvedanta.org), built in 1906. In line with its mission "to promote harmony between Eastern and Western thought, and recognition of the truth in all the great religions of the world," each of the temple's unique towers represents a different major world religious tradition. It is thought to be the first Hindu temple built in the West.

UNION STREET

From the temple, return to Union Street and turn left into the heart of yuppie Cow Hollow, named for the cow pastures and dairy-farming industry that once dominated the area. At No. 2040, the old farmhouse of dairy rancher **James Cudworth ⑫** stands as evidence from that era.

Nearby at No. 1980 are the wedding presents Cudworth built for his daughters: a pair of identical Victorians known as the **Wedding Houses ⑬** that share a front porch. Today, Cow Hollow brims with boutiques, trendy eateries, and singles-scene bars frequented by preppy young professionals.

If you need nourishment, stop at one of the many eateries clustered along Union Street, including **Rose's Café ❸**, **Gamine ❹**, and **Umami Burger ❺**.

Union Street

Octagon House

OCTAGON HOUSE

Turn right on Gough Street and end the tour at the quaint, eight-sided building, the **Octagon House** ⓮ (No. 2645; tel: 441-7512; Feb–Dec 2nd Sun of month, 2nd and 4th Thur of month noon–3pm; donation appreciated). Popular in the mid-19th century, eight-sided houses (like the Feusier House, see page 62) were advocated for their health benefits, namely increased sunlight and better ventilation afforded by the cupola. Built in 1861 by William C. McElroy and now a San Francisco Historical Landmark, the cottage-like structure looks like it has popped out of a fairy tale; it is painted a pale blue, frosted with white trimming, and framed by a picket fence. Inside are items of period furniture, documents, and decorative arts.

Food and Drink

❶ LA BOULANGE AT FILLMORE

2043 Fillmore Street; tel: 928-1300; www.baybread.com; daily 7am–6pm; $
Just around the corner from the original, "mother" bakery, La Boulangerie (2325 Pine Street), this spot delights with flaky French pastries, organic coffee and espresso, open-faced sandwiches, and old-fashioned burgers.

❷ ELITE CAFÉ

2049 Fillmore Street; tel: 346-8668; Mon–Fri D only, Sat–Sun Br and D; $$
This tried-and-true locals' fave serves Cajun- and Creole-inspired seafood dishes in a cheery atmosphere. An excellent raw bar beckons, as does the Cajun brunch, with perfectly seasoned Bloody Marys.

❸ ROSE'S CAFE

2298 Union Street, tel: 775-2200; www.rosescafesf.com; daily B, L & D; $$
Rose's has been a neighborhood go-to for over 15 years, delivering fresh and simple Italian-inspired fare in a friendly, casual setting. On weekends, an outdoor table is the perfect place to people watch over brunch.

❹ GAMINE

2223 Union Street, tel: 771-7771; www.gaminesf.com; daily D; $$
Come hungry to this cozy and convivial French bistro, and feast on baked cambazola, mussels, escargots, onion soup, or a burger topped with brie and an egg.

❺ UMAMI BURGER

2184 Union Street, tel: 440-8626; www.unami.com; daily L & D; $$
If you're craving an amazing burger with creative toppings – think housemade truffle cheese and truffle glaze, or shitake mushrooms, caramelized onions, and Parmesan crisps – Umami Burger won't disappoint.

Sphinx sculpture outside the de Young Museum

GOLDEN GATE PARK AND HAIGHT-ASHBURY

Golden Gate Park is perfect for whiling away time out of doors, filled with fields, gardens, and lakes and home to the de Young Museum. Haight Street, meanwhile, is a counterculture landmark cluttered with thrift shops and cheap eateries.

DISTANCE: 3 miles (5km)
TIME: A full day
START: de Young Museum
END: Haight-Ashbury
POINTS TO NOTE: Although Golden Gate Park is immense, do not worry too much about getting lost in the wilderness. Paths are well marked, with signs and maps pointing you in the direction of various major attractions. This route begins at the de Young Museum. The 5 and 21 buses stop at 8th and Fulton streets, just outside the park. Walk into the park and turn right on John F. Kennedy Drive to reach the museum's tower entrance. To return downtown from the Haight, take the 7 or 71 buses that run along the full length of Haight Street, or the 6, which makes its first stop on Haight at Masonic.

One of San Francisco's icons, Golden Gate Park represents the late-19th-century aspirations of civic leaders who sought to build a city (and a park) riva-

ling New York. Haight-Ashbury, on the other hand, came to represent the aspirations of the hippie movement, whose roots lay in the countercultural values of the Beat Generation.

GOLDEN GATE PARK

Where rolling sand dunes could once be seen, Golden Gate Park's grassy hills now carpet over 1,000 acres (405 hectares) of land that stretches 52 blocks from the edge of the Haight-Ashbury neighborhood to the Pacific Ocean. Surrounded by gardens and groves, it is easy to forget about the hustle and bustle of the city, especially on Sundays, when John F. Kennedy Drive is closed to car traffic. Sporty people converge on the park to take advantage of fields and miles of trails to run and bike along, not to mention the golf course, polo and archery fields, tennis courts, and fly-fishing pond. Others picnic, barbeque, and nap on the lawns.

The park is also home to 11 lakes, the largest of which is Stow Lake, in the western part of the park. There you can

The de Young Museum café   *The lake in Golden Gate Park*

rent rowboats and paddle boats (tel: 752-0347; charge) and spend a leisurely afternoon gliding around with the turtles

De Young Museum

In 2005, the **de Young Museum ❶** (50 Hagiwara Tea Garden Drive; www. deyoung.famsf.org; Tue–Sun 9.30am–5.15pm, Fri until 8.45pm; charge, 1st Tue of month free) reopened in Golden Gate Park in a bold facility that replaced the one severely damaged by the 1989 Loma Prieta earthquake. The controversial design features a copper-clad exterior that will oxidize over time and a nine-story observation tower that sticks out (literally and figuratively) in the natural park setting. From the top of the de Young's twisting 144ft (44m) copper observation tower, the amazing panorama of San Francisco's cityscape is as stunning a work of art as any you might find inside the museum. On a clear day,

the 360-degree floor-to-ceiling windows reveal the city in all its glory.

Several fine collections are displayed in the spacious, light-filled interior: the concourse level hosts 20th-century and contemporary art (including works by Georgia O'Keeffe, Edward Hopper, and Grant Wood), art from the Americas, Native American art, and a room of murals, while upstairs are rare works from Africa, Oceania, and New Guinea, plus early American artworks and separate textile and photography exhibits.

The museum also has a sculpture garden, museum store, and café, and mounts immensely popular special exhibitions, featuring works from the likes of photographer Annie Leibovitz and glass artist Dale Chihuly.

Japanese Tea Garden

Just west of the de Young along Hagiwara Tea Garden Drive is the **Japanese Tea Garden ❷** (www.japanese

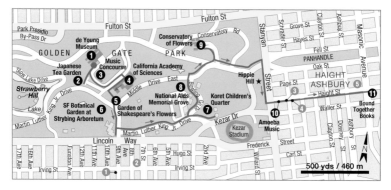

Garden of Shakespeare's Flowers

teagardensf.com; daily 9am–6pm; charge). This peaceful setting of cherry blossoms, bonsai conifers, carp ponds, and wooden bridges is the oldest public Japanese-style garden in the country, and a popular place to wander and snack on tea and cookies sold in the garden's teahouse.

California Academy of Sciences
Cross the 20,000-seat **Music Concourse** ❸ – an outdoor summer music venue completed in 1900 and landscaped with fountains and trees – to reach the **California Academy of Sciences** ❹ (55 Music Concourse Drive; www.calacademy.org; Mon–Sat 9.30am–5pm, Sun 11am–5pm;

charge, 3rd Wed of month free). The academy reopened in Golden Gate Park after much anticipation. Italian-born Pritzker Prize-winning architect Renzo Piano designed the structure, which integrates the architecture with the park's natural setting through sustainable features such as a living roof, solar panels, and water reclamation. The interactive natural history museum boasts a collection of some 18 million scientific specimens, including plants, animals, fossils, and artifacts. The Steinhart Aquarium is home to a bright array of exotic fish and other swimming and slithering species. Also on site are a live coral reef and a large natural history collection from the Galápagos Islands.

Garden of Shakespeare's Flowers
Exit the Academy on Music Concourse Drive and turn left on Martin Luther King Jr. Drive. Turn left again into the **Garden of Shakespeare's Flowers** ❺, a collection of flowers and herbs that are mentioned in poems and plays penned by the bard, accompanied by plaques at one end of the garden that are engraved with relevant quotations.

San Francisco Botanical Garden
Continue south on Martin Luther King Jr. Drive to reach the **San Francisco Botanical Garden at Strybing Arboretum** ❻ (9th Avenue and Lincoln Way; www.sfbotanicalgarden.org; Nov–Jan 7.30am–4pm, Feb–Mar 7.30am–5pm, Apr–Sep 7.30am–6pm, Oct 7.30am–

Park Superintendents

At the entrance to the McLaren Memorial Rhododendron Dell, just west of the Conservatory of Flowers on John F. Kennedy Drive, you will see a prominent, life-sized statue of "Uncle John" McLaren, the canny park superintendent for 53 years (1890–1943). The statue, erected after his death, is more than a little ironic: the Scotsman notoriously detested statues and deliberately hid those in the park with dense foliage. Though McLaren is the best-known park superintendent, famous for the work he completed during his tenure, he was not the first. That distinction goes to William Hammond Hall from 1871–86.

Conservatory of Flowers

5pm; charge, free 7.30–9am daily and second Tue every month). From Mediterranean to tropical cloud-forest plants, the 7,500 diverse species found here come from all around the globe. A "Garden of Fragrance" is one of several specialty gardens, and free guided walks are offered daily at 1.30pm. Alternatively, join the multitudes that choose the grass outside the Arboretum in which to relax and soak up the sun.

Koret Children's Quarter

Walk east on Martin Luther King Jr. for about a mile. If you are hungry, turn right on 7th Avenue for lunch options in the Inner Sunset neighborhood. Feast on gourmet pizza at **Arizmendi** ❶ or Indian cuisine at **Naan 'n' Curry** ❷, or choose from one of the many other eateries on Irving Street. Return to Martin Luther King Jr. Drive, pass the baseball diamonds on your left, and enter the historic **Koret Children's Quarter** ❼.

Formerly known as the Children's Playground, this public playground built in 1887 is oldest in the U.S. Nearby, youngsters ride on the colorful carrousel (charge), which was carved in 1912 and was one of the main carrousels at the 1939 World's Fair on San Francisco's Treasure Island. Look north and you will see **Hippie Hill**, home to ad hoc musical celebrations on weekends, with dozens of locals letting loose with drums, shakers, or whatever else they can find, from pans

to sticks. Hula-hoops and roller skates are optional.

National Aids Memorial Grove

Walk west to and head north along Bowling Green Drive; at its intersection with Middle Drive East is the main portal of the **National Aids Memorial Grove** ❽ (www.aidsmemorial. org; free). Over seven wooded acres (3 hectares) comprise this peaceful, living tribute to those whose lives have been affected either directly or indirectly by AIDS. Follow the Woodland Path access ramp, and pass through the redwoods to arrive at the Circle of Friends monument.

Conservatory of Flowers

Walk up Middle Drive East and cross John F. Kennedy Drive to reach the bright-white and beautifully landscaped **Conservatory of Flowers** ❾ (www.conservatoryofflowers.org; Tue–Sun 10am–4.30pm; charge except first Tue of month). Built in the late 1870s, the elegant, glass-domed structure was modeled after the Palm House in England's Kew Gardens. Vibrantly colored tropical flowers are the main focus of five galleries overflowing with nearly 2,000 plant species. A highland tropics exhibit nurtures a renowned collection of high-altitude orchids amid climbing vines, moss-carpeted rocks, and a profusion of ferns. In the pool-filled aquatic plants exhibit, feast your eyes on carnivorous plants

Painting in the park

Haight-Ashbury History

Filled with grand Victorians and large backyards, Haight-Ashbury began as a suburb that was linked by the Haight Street Cable Railroad to the Financial District. In the housing shortage during World War II, many of these single homes were divided into apartments, which were vacated once the war was over, as families left for the suburbs in the 1950s mass "white flight."

Low rents initially attracted the next wave of bohemians that followed the Beats of North Beach. By the mid-1960s, the neighborhood had filled with head shops, boutiques, bookstores, musicians, and artists. In 1966, at the intersection of Haight and Ashbury streets a young, clean-shaven Jerry Garcia posed with the rest of the Grateful Dead for one of the era's iconic photos, proclaiming the district to be the epicenter of the quickly emerging counterculture. But it was in 1967 when the neighborhood truly gained iconic status, as tens of thousands flocked here for first the "Human Be-In" and then the famous "Summer of Love." The Summer of Love kick-started the careers of San Francisco bands such as Jefferson Airplane and Big Brother and the Holding Company, not to mention the Grateful Dead, whose former home is one block south of Haight Street at 710 Ashbury Street (now a private home).

and giant Victoria amazonica water lilies that can reach 6ft (2m) in diameter. The Dahlia Garden decorates the eastern side of the conservatory, while in the spring, 850 varieties of rhododendron bloom in the McLaren Memorial Rhododendron Dell to the west. Walk east on John F. Kennedy Drive to exit the park, turning right on Stanyan left on Haight Street.

HAIGHT-ASHBURY

While "The Haight," as locals call it, is steeped in nostalgia, there are plenty of modern-day hipsters and "hippie" homeless types claiming the neighborhood as their own. The Upper Haight, roughly from Stanyan to Masonic streets, is a mishmash of thrift stores, hip boutiques, cheap eateries, friendly local bars, independent music stores, and bookshops. The neighborhood is plagued by persistent panhandlers, and the grungy feel becomes grittier descending into the Lower Haight (between Divisadero and Webster), but a laid-back atmosphere prevails: most stores open after 11am (or noon on weekends), and the morning traffic rush only starts in the middle of the day.

Haight Street

Stroll east on Haight Street to take in the varied funky shops. **Amoeba Music** ❿ (No. 1855; www.amoeba. com) is a progressive independent

No mistaking the neighborhood　　　　　*Victorian architecture in Haight–Ashbury*

music seller housed in a converted bowling alley, with especially fine experimental offerings in rock, hip-hop, electronica, and jazz.

For a dose of "subversive" literature, pop into **Bound Together Books** ⓫ (No. 1369; www.boundtogetherbooks.word press.com). This volunteer-run bookstore sells anarchist and other non- tra- ditional literature, and the side of the building features a colorful mural by local artist Susan Greene depicting famous anarchists.

End your route with a meal at one of the Haight's casual and diverse eateries, such as tapas bar **Cha Cha Cha** ❸, *taquería* **Zona Rosa** ❹, or *crêperie* **Squat and Gobble** ❺.

Food and Drink

❶ ARIZMENDI
1331 9th Avenue; tel: 566-3117; www.arizmendibakery.com; Tue–Sun B, L, and D; $
Two blocks from Golden Gate Park, this worker-owned bakery serves up a different gourmet pizza every day – think artichoke hearts, red onions, asiago cheese, and garlic oil; or carmelized onions, ricotta cheese, and basil pesto. The thin sourdough crust, however, stays constant. Freshly baked morning breads and pastries also rotate daily.

❷ NAAN 'N' CURRY
642 Irving Street; tel: 664-7225; daily L and D; $
So much flavor for so little cash. This Inner Sunset location is one of several Indian/ Pakistani eateries known for its delicious food and low prices. Short on decor but long on spiciness, the chicken vindaloo, tikka masala and tandoori all hit the mark.

❸ CHA CHA CHA
1801 Haight Street; tel: 386-5758; daily L and D; $
Smack dab in the middle of Haight-Ashbury, Cha Cha Cha is a fun place for tapas, Caribbean-inspired entrees, and potent sangria. The crowd is young, hip, and noisy.

❹ ZONA ROSA
1797 Haight Street; tel: 668-7717; daily L and D; $; cash only
Craving a burrito but too weary to go all the way to the Mission? This groovy *taquería* is good for a quick bite in a quirky setting. Vegetarian options are particularly popular.

❺ SQUAT AND GOBBLE
1428 Haight Street; tel: 864-8484; www.squatandgobble.com; daily B and L; $
Yummy and consistent chain with a large open-air patio out back. Pick from sweet and savory crepes served with rosemary garlic potatoes, or from scrambled eggs, sandwiches, and salads, then take your time gobbling, and enjoying the casual, friendly atmosphere.

LGBT-friendly district

THE CASTRO

Enjoy truly "good views" from the wooded and steeply sloping Buena Vista Park. Then walk the tidy streets of the rainbow-flag-festooned Castro District, one of the city's most vibrant, diverse, and politically active districts.

DISTANCE: 2 miles (3km)
TIME: A half-day
START: Buena Vista Park
END: Castro and 16th streets
POINTS TO NOTE: This tour of the Castro begins at the entrance to Buena Vista Park at Haight Street and Central Avenue. To reach this starting point, take bus 6, 43, 66, or 71. This tour is a good one to do in the afternoon into evening, so consider doing it after walk 11.

The well-groomed Castro, considered by many to be the gay capital of the world, showcases beautifully restored Victorian and Edwardian homes, while draping its thriving nightlife, love of shopping, and political activism in rainbow flags.

BUENA VISTA PARK

Dating from 1867, **Buena Vista Park** ❶ is San Francisco's oldest park. When the city converted its many cemeteries into parks, workers were ordered to use the unclaimed headstones for the new trails and gutters. Out of respect for the dead, many decided to leave the pieces facing upwards; some of these are still visible today in Buena Vista Park.

Walk southwest along the steep sidewalk of Buena Vista Avenue West, which clings to the park's edge, passing grand and beautifully restored Victorians. One of these, at No. 737, is the picturesque **Spreckels Mansion** ❷ (not to be confused with the mansion of the same name in Pacific Heights). Built in the late 19th century for sugarmagnate Richard Spreckels, the now private residence was also once home to Ambrose Bierce and Jack London.

Buena Vista Avenue West becomes Buena Vista Avenue East, turning sharply northeast. Take the path into the park here for breathtaking downtown views. Then continue on Buena Vista Avenue East, turning right on Buena Vista Terrace, left on 14th Street, and right on Castro Street, descending to Market Street and the colorful center of the Castro.

Castro Street   *The Baroque façade of Castro Theatre*

THE CASTRO DISTRICT

It was only 30 years ago that the Castro shifted from a working-class, Irish Catholic neighborhood to the city's thriving, politically active gay hub, but it is hard now to imagine it any differently. San Francisco is often referred to as the gay capital of the world, a title its residents wear with pride. The active lesbian and gay community that has made its home in the Castro has contributed significantly to every area of San Francisco's culture: economic, artistic, and political. Today, the tightly knit community is safe, well maintained, and filled with friendly eateries, unique shops, and brightly colored Victorians and Edwardians.

Harvey Milk Plaza

At the intersection of Castro and Market streets is **Harvey Milk Plaza ❸**. Harvey Milk was a Castro Street camera shop owner and gay activist who organized the area's merchants' group. In 1977, he was elected to the Board of Supervisors, becoming the first openly gay city official to be elected in American politics. In 1978, former supervisor Dan White, the city's most anti-gay politician, shot and killed Milk and Mayor George Moscone in their City Hall offices. The city reeled in shock, and a somber, mixed crowd marched from Castro Street to Ctiy Hall, silently bearing candles. Six months later, a jury sentenced White to just 5 years, with White avoiding a murder conviction with the infamous "Twinkie Defense," which claimed a sugar high had reduced White's mental capacity. The lenient sentence provoked enraged protestors to descend on City Hall in the White Night Riot of May 21, 1979, torching the capitol and police cars. White, paroled in 1985, committed suicide in the same year that *The Life and Times of Harvey*

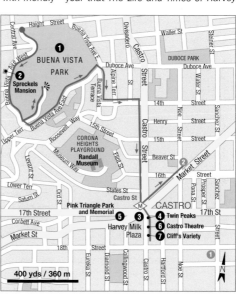

Orphan Andy's 24-hour restaurant

Milk won an Oscar for best documentary. In 2008, Sean Penn portrayed Harvey Milk in the biographical drama *Milk*.

Here also is historic **Twin Peaks ❹** (401 Castro Street; www.twinpeaks tavern.com; Mon–Wed noon–2am, Thur–Sun 8am–2am), a friendly neighborhood tavern and the country's first openly gay bar.

Just to the west of this intersection, an island wedge between Market and 17th streets hosts the **Pink Triangle Park and Memorial ❺** (http://pinktrianglepark. org). The 15,000 or so gays, lesbians, bisexuals, and transgenders who were persecuted during and following the Nazi regime are commemorated here by 15 white-granite pylons inlaid with pink triangles (the symbol once worn by LGBT concentration-camp prisoners) and positioned in the shape of a triangle.

Castro Theatre

Castro Street, between 17th and 19th streets, is the neighborhood's compact commercial center, packed with stores, bars, cafés, and restaurants. Head south on Castro Street for the **Castro Theatre ❻** (No. 429; www.castrotheatre. com). This ornate yet intimate Spanish Baroque theater, complete with Art Deco flourishes, was built in 1922 and designated a U.S. National Landmark in 1977. The revival movie house new releases, independent films, musical sing-a-longs (*Sound of Music*, *Grease*, *Mary Poppins*), and film festivals, and on special nights a live organist plays on a platform that ascends before the start of the film.

Cliff's Variety

Continue south on Castro. This tightly packed commercial strip largely caters to the gay community and is devoid of retail chains. Instead, look for quirky longtime neighborhood outposts such as **Cliff's Variety ❼** (479 Castro Street; www. cliffsvariety.com; Mon–Fri 9am–8pm, Sat 9.30am–8pm, Sun 11am–6pm), a unique hardware store with aisles of tools, craft supplies, fancy-dress outfits, and home-decoration items.

To end the walk, turn left on 18th Street and walk 3 blocks to **Samovar Tea Lounge ❶**, or return to Market Street and turn right to recharge at **Café Flore ❷**.

Food and Drink

❶ SAMOVAR TEA LOUNGE

498 Sanchez Street; tel: 626-4700; www. samovarlife.com; daily 10am–10pm; $
Rest and recover while sipping small-batch artisan teas paired with international dishes. Private tea classes are also offered.

❷ CAFÉ FLORE

2298 Market Street; tel: 621-8579; www.cafeflore.com; daily B, L, and D; $
The diverse crowds that frequent this ever-bustling intersection make this café perfect for people-watching. Order your coffee, *frittata*, or sandwich at the counter and grab a table on the sunny patio.

Mission Dolores

THE MISSION DISTRICT

The Mission District is one of the city's most dynamic, diverse neighborhoods. It is home to a large working-class Latino population as well as artists and hipsters and, increasingly, young tech workers.

DISTANCE: 2.5 miles (4km)
TIME: A half-day
START: Mission Dolores
END: 24th Street
POINTS TO NOTE: This district is best explored by day. To reach the starting point by public transport, take bus: 22, 26, or F, or Metro: J, K, L, M, T to Church station.

The Mission is one of the oldest parts of San Francisco, inhabited by Ohlone Indians for over 2,000 years before Spanish missionaries arrived in the mid-18th century. The area remained remote from the first center of town, Portsmouth Square, until the mid-1850s when large Irish and German working-class immigrant populations settled here. Another wave of development followed the 1906 earthquake, when the neighborhood welcomed displaced residents and businesses. The area's Latin character began in the 1940s–60s with a growing Mexican community, who were joined in the 1980s and 1990s by immigrants and refugees fleeing Central and South America. Today, in addition to the Latino community, young hipsters and techies also call the Mission home. On weekends they swarm Dolores Park, and help kick off the boisterous nightlife scene in the neighborhood when the sun sets.

MISSION DOLORES

Begin at the intersection of 16th and Dolores streets for **Mission Dolores** ❶, more formally known as Misión San Francisco de Asís (3321 16th Street; www.missiondolores.org; daily 9am–4pm; donation suggested). Built in 1776, this narrow adobe church was sixth in the chain of 21 Spanish missions that stretched 650 miles (1,000km) along the California coast from San Diego to northern California. Completed just days before the signing of the Declaration of Independence in 1776, it is the oldest intact building in the city. The church was dedicated to San Francisco de Assisi, but became known as Mission Dolores, probably because of the small

Stained glass window, Mission Dolores

lagoon on which it was built, Nuestra Señora de los Dolores.

Over the centuries the stout mission building's 4ft (1m) -thick adobe walls have withstood numerous natural disasters. The original bells, cast in the 1790s, hang from leather thongs above the vestibule, and most of the original craftwork is intact. Carved Mexican altars stand at the head of the interior, and a restored ceiling is decorated with colorful Ohlone Indian designs. Outside, in the peaceful cemetery, over 5,000 Costanoan Native Americans are buried amidst traditional native trees, shrubs, flowers, and plants. With them are some of the first Californians and pioneers who gave their names to San Francisco streets, including Don Luis Antonio Arguello, the first governor of Alta California under Mexican rule.

16TH STREET

Walk east along arty 16th Street. **Needles & Pens ②** (No. 3253; www.needles-pens.com; daily noon–7pm) doubles up as an art gallery and purveyor of zines, art-books, locally made jewelry, and music. At No. 3245 sits **Creativity Explored ③** (www.creativityexplored.org; studio: Mon–Fri 8.30am–2.30pm, gallery: Mon–Fri 10am–3pm (Thur until 7pm), Sat–Sun noon–5pm), a nonprofit visual-arts center where artists with developmental disabilities create, exhibit, and sell art. Next up is **The Roxie ④** (No. 3117; www.roxie.com), an art-house cinema with a reputation for risk-taking programs – its roster of rare and experimental films are anything but mainstream. The larger auditorium is considered the second-oldest continually run cinema in the country.

THE WOMEN'S BUILDING

For a burrito break, continue on 16th to **Pancho Villa ①**, then head south on Valencia Street. Turn right on 17th and then left on Dearborn, a charming residential block with a community garden. Ahead, across 18th Street is the **Women's Building ⑤** (3543 18th Street; www.womensbuilding.org; daily 9am–5pm, additional evening hours vary), a "multi-ethnic, multi-cultural, multi-service center for women and girls," with a bold and beautiful *Maestra Peace* mural on its outer walls.

MISSION DOLORES PARK

Head west along 18th Street and turn left on Guerrero Street to grab a coffee and some melt-in-your-mouth pastries at **Tartine Bakery ②**, or continue walking to reach the corner of 18th and Dolores and **Mission Dolores Park ⑥**, one of the sunniest spots in the city and huge social scene on pleasant weekends. Frisky dogs and energetic ballplayers get their exercise, while picnickers sun themselves, flirt, and enjoy

Balmy Alley murals	*The Baroque dome of the Mission High School*

the city views (which are best at the corner near 20th and Church streets). Exit the park onto Dolores Street, head east on 19th Street, and then south back onto Valencia Street.

VALENCIA STREET

As the creative, eclectic center of the Mission, Valencia Street is filled with independent bookstores, quirky shops and thrift stores, and hip eateries and bars. Walk south on Valencia to **Paxton Gate ❼** (No. 824; www.paxtongate.com), where you'll find terrariums, taxidermy items, and other unconventional items inspired by gardens and natural sciences. Next door is 826 **Valencia ❽** (www.826valencia.org; daily noon–6pm), a youth literary center co-founded by local literary talent Dave Eggers. Somewhat bizarrely,

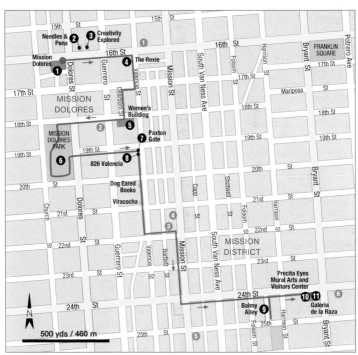

El Capitan Theatre, Mission Street

826 Valencia also doubles as a Pirate Supply Store, filled with eye patches, message bottles, spyglasses, and other pirate paraphernalia. Continue on to **Dog Eared Books** (900 Valencia Street; www.dogearedbooks.com), a new and used bookstore specializing in Beat, off-beat, small press, and local literature. One block further takes you to **Viracocha** (998 Valencia Street; http://viracochasf.com), an antiques shop selling typewriters, books, and clothes.

MISSION STREET

Turn left on 22nd Street. If you need a break at this point, join the local artists and musicians at **Revolution Café** ❸. Turn right on Mission Street, passing choice dinner spots such as Foreign Cinema ❹. Rougher around the edges than Valencia, Mission Street is lined with discount shops, outlets for inexpensive clothes, pawn brokers, Mexican grocery stores, bars, and diners. The numerous Art Deco marquees speak of a more prosperous time, but the street is still rich in culture, albeit rather less salubrious after dark. For a change of taste, pick up a slice of something sweet or savory at **Mission Pie** ❺.

24TH STREET

Turn east on 24th Street, known as *El Corazón de la Misión* (the Heart of the Mission). The Latino culture for which the Mission is famous is especially evident in this area: in particular, the stretch of 24th Street from Mission to Folsom is lined with trees and peppered with *taquerías*, mural-adorned alleys, and art organizations.

Balmy Alley

Turn right onto **Balmy Alley** ❾, where murals depicting scenes from life in the Mission or in Central American villages cover almost every wall. Murals throughout the Mission – painted on bare walls, on buildings, and inside or outside restaurants – express its political consciousness as well as a deep connection to *La Raza* (the race, or the people).

Guided tours of the murals in this area are conducted by the **Precita Eyes Mural Arts and Visitors Center** ❿ (2981 24th Street; www.precitaeyes. org; center: Mon–Fri 10am–5pm, Sat 10am–4pm, Sun noon–4pm, tours: check website for details of walks currently offered; charge). It also offers lots of information about the Mission's colorful murals and has a store that sells gifts and art supplies. A free Mission murals tour is also offered several times a month by San Francisco City Guides (www.sfcityguides.org).

Galería de la Raza

Further along 24th Street is **Galería de la Raza** ⓫ (No. 2857; www.galeria delaraza.org; Tue 1–7pm, Wed–Sat

Dolores Park　　　　　　　　　　　　　　*A colorful Mission mural*

noon–6pm, but call to confirm hours; free), a mixed space for art and activism that celebrates Chicano and Latino art and culture. Founded in 1970, it is largely considered the most important Chicano art center in the country. Having had your fill of art and culture, you can now end the route with a satisfying meal at **St Francis Fountain** ❺.

Food and Drink

❶ PANCHO VILLA

3071 16th Street; tel: 864-8840; daily L and D; $

Here it is: the world-renowned San Francisco burrito. Pancho Villa is counter service only, and incredibly inexpensive. Have a late lunch and you will not need dinner.

❷ TARTINE BAKERY

600 Guerrero Street; tel: 487-2600; www.tartinebakery.com; daily B, L, and D; $

Locals drool over the eclairs, tarts, freshly baked bread and other treats from this small bakery and café. For something more substantial, try a croque-monsieur or a pressed sandwich, accompanied by wine or organic coffee.

❸ REVOLUTION CAFÉ

3248 22nd Street; tel: 642-0474; daily B, L, and D; $

This French-style café is a friendly gathering place for artists, musicians, and other bohemian types, who enjoy chatting in the down-to-earth atmosphere and, some nights, listening to live classical and jazz music while drinking wine and beer. Indoor and outdoor seating available.

❹ FOREIGN CINEMA

2534 Mission Street; tel: 648-7600; www.foreigncinema.com; D daily, Br Sat–Sun $$$

Dinner and a movie gets a new spin at this popular, industrial-chic eatery. Innovative California cuisine can be enjoyed inside by the fire, or better yet, dine on the heated outdoor courtyard where movies are screened on a concrete wall.

❺ MISSION PIE

2901 Mission Street; tel: 282-1500; www.missionpie.com; daily B, L, and D; $

Banana cream, walnut, strawberry rhubarb, pear blueberry – the sweet pies at this corner café and bakery are just divine. For something savory, try their pot pies and galettes.

❻ ST FRANCIS FOUNTAIN

2801 24th Street; tel: 826-4200; daily B, L, and D; $$

Family-owned since 1918, this pink-walled 1940s-style soda fountain serves up classic ice cream desserts and house-made candy as well as hearty breakfasts, burger and sandwiches, and daily specials.

GGNRA headquarters

FORT MASON AND THE MARINA

This walk takes you from old Fort Mason to the Palace of Fine Arts before winding inland to reach Chestnut Street, the Marina's upscale commercial thoroughfare.

DISTANCE: 3 miles (5km)
TIME: A half-day
START: Fort Mason
END: Chestnut Street
POINTS TO NOTE: From the start of Marina Boulevard, the wave organ is a 1-mile (1.6km) round trip. The tour begins at Marina Boulevard and Laguna Street at the entrance to Fort Mason (Metro: F to the Embarcadero and Stockton Street; bus: 10, 15).

Dating back to the Civil War period, Fort Mason is now the north shore's culture capital; its piers and buildings host all manner of performances and recreational activities. The Marina neighborhood in which it is found is popular with young professionals, who make good money in the Financial District and pack out the local bars at the weekend.

FORT MASON

A military base for over 200 years, the 13-acre (5-hectare) waterfront of

Fort Mason ❶ (www.fortmason.org) once served as an embarkation point for troops and supplies headed to the Pacific during the World War II and the Korean conflict. In 1977, Fort Mason was transformed into a cultural center, and the Mission Revival buildings house non-profit organizations and host 15,000 events each year. Fort Mason also houses the headquarters of the Golden Gate National Recreational Area (GGNRA; www.nps.gov/goga), a national park that stretches across 28 miles (45km) of coastline in San Francisco, Marin, and San Mateo counties. It includes major attractions such as Alcatraz, the Presidio, Muir Woods, and the Marin Headlands.

Center highlights

The lofty, light-filled **SFMOMA Artists Gallery** (Fort Mason Building A; www.sfmoma.org; Tue–Sat 10.30am–5pm; free) shows sculpture, painting, photography, and mixed-media work from Northern California artists, and has an art-rental program that allows art aficionados to test out artwork (sculpture,

Marina small craft harbor   *Restaurants on Chestnut Street*

paintings, photography, mixed media, etc.) in their own home, with an option to buy. Building D houses the **Magic Theater**, which has premiered works by Pulitzer Prize-winners Sam Shepard and David Mamet and innovative pieces by emerging playwrights.

The small permanent collection at **Museo Italo-Americano** ❷ (Fort Mason Building C; www.museoitaloamericano. org; Mon by appointment, Tue–Sun noon–4pm; free) features paintings, sculptures, photographs, and works on paper by prominent Italian and Italian-American artists.

Pop into **Greens** ❶ for tasty vegetarian food with harbor views; alter-

natively, choose from the selection of sandwiches or salads at their take-out counter and enjoy a picnic on Marina Green.

YACHT HARBOR TO THE WAVE ORGAN

Exit Fort Mason through the western parking lot, hugging the coast past **Gaslight Cove** ❸ (also known as the East Harbor), one of the Marina's two yacht harbors. Follow the shoreline promenade along the long and lovely **Marina Green** ❹, sandwiched between the bay and Marina Boulevard. The flat, scenic stretch in an oth-

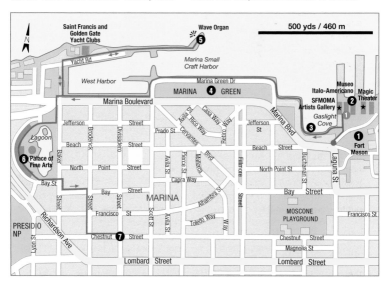

The Palace of Fine Arts

erwise hilly city is a year-round favorite of walkers, joggers, picnickers, and kite-fliers, and on the Fourth of July attracts hoards of fireworks viewers.

The Wave Organ

For a unique view of both the Golden Gate Bridge and the city's northern shore, veer right onto Yacht Road and follow it round the West Harbor, passing the Saint Francis and Golden Gate yacht clubs. At the end of the rocky jetty is the **Wave Organ 5**, an acoustic sculpture comprising 25 organ pipes. Sea water swelling in and out causes the pipes to emit subtle tones. Try to visit at high tide to hear them at their best. Enjoy picturesque views of the Golden Gate Bridge, then retrace your steps and cross Marina Boulevard.

PALACE OF FINE ARTS

The **Palace of Fine Arts 6** was built for the 288-day Panama-Pacific International Exposition of 1915, a world's fair that celebrated the completion of the Panama Canal and (unofficially) San Francisco's rebound from the 1906 disaster. Designed by Bernard Maybeck, the stunning Beaux Arts structure, with massive colonnades and imposing rotunda, was originally made of plaster and was reconstructed out of concrete in the 1960s.

Today the Palace hosts occasional events and art exhibitions, and is a popular spot for wedding photographs. Take a break on the bench-lined lawns, watching swans swim across the mirror-like lagoon, then walk south on Baker Street to turn left on Bay Street, right on Broderick Street, and finally left on Chestnut Street.

CHESTNUT STREET

Chestnut Street 7 is the main commercial thoroughfare of the Marina District, and caters to a fairly homogeneous crowd of well-to-do young professionals who frequent the upscale restaurants, mainstream home-and-beauty retailers, glossy boutiques, and happening singles bars.

Food and Drink

① GREENS

Building A, Fort Mason Center; tel: 771-6222; www.greensrestaurant.com; Mon D only, Tue–Sat L and D, Sun Br and D; $$$

This airy, upscale vegetarian restaurant is located in a former army warehouse with a beautiful bayside setting. It serves savory fare that even non-veggies rave about, from filled filo pastries to mesquite-grilled vegetable brochettes. Reservations are recommended. If the restaurant's full and you fancy a picnic, you can always try the take-out counter, Greens to Go, which is open all day.

The Golden Gate Bridge seen from Baker Beach

GOLDEN GATE PROMENADE

This straight seaside ramble runs along the restored tidal marshland of Crissy Field to the historic Fort Point at the base of the Golden Gate Bridge. Continue along the bridge for stellar views back over the city.

DISTANCE: 2.5 miles (4km)
TIME: 2 hours
START: Crissy Field
END: Fort Point
POINTS TO NOTE: Fort Point is closed Mon–Thur. A wide, fully accessible trail is convenient for wheelchairs and strollers. For a quieter and less blustery walk, do this tour in the early morning, as the wind generally picks up by mid-day. To get within four blocks of the tour's starting point, take the 30 bus to Broderick and Jefferson streets. To return downtown from Fort Point, take the 28 bus to the Marina and transfer to the 30.

Perhaps the most photographed bridge in the world, the iconic Golden Gate Bridge, painted in "International Orange," is certainly one of the world's most famous. Numerous movies have featured it as a backdrop or contain scenes filmed on the bridge (see page 22). No trip to the city is complete without at least a visit to its base if not a walk or drive across it.

GOLDEN GATE PROMENADE

Begin at Yacht Road, north of Marina Boulevard. Head northwards along the bayfront promenade, enjoying stiff, salty breezes as you ramble along **Crissy Field ❶**, a restored tidal marshland with 22 acres (9 hectares) of dunes. It was once the airfield of the Presidio army base, and was named

Food and Drink

❶ WARMING HUT

983 Marine Drive; daily 9am–5pm; $
The bright café is the perfect place to rest and recharge after a windblown walk along Crissy Field. Get toasty with a hot cup of coffee, fresh pastries, sandwiches, and other offerings with an emphasis on fresh, organic ingredients. Then browse the store selling books and gifts with an environmental theme.

Fort Point

after military aviator Major Dana H. Crissy. With its flat, tidy trail and great views, it is a popular spot with locals and visitors alike, who come to walk, run, and bike, or simply to relax with a picnic and watch the expert windsurfing and parasailing taking place at the East Beach. You can also legally fish or crab without a license at Torpedo Wharf at the west end of Crissy Field. Look for posted regulations.

Crissy Field is also part of the 1,491-acre (603-hectare) **Presidio** (bordered by Lyon Street and West Pacific Avenue; www.nps.gov/prsf; free). A military post for over 200 years, the Presidio today is a shoreline park boasting beaches, cliffs, woods, historical sites, a golf course, a lake, 14 miles (23km) of paved roads, and 11 miles (18km) of hiking trails.

FORT POINT

At the intersection of Long Avenue and Marine Drive are the administrative offices of Fort Point (Marine Drive; www.nps.gov/fopo; Fri–Sun 10am–5pm). Here you may take a break at the **Warming Hut ❶**, and smooth your windblown hair. Follow Marine Drive to its end to reach **Fort Point ❷**, a massive structure that's been called the "the pride of the Pacific," "the Gibraltar of the West Coast," and "one of the most perfect models of masonry in America."

Fort Point is significant for its military and maritime history as well as its architecture. Built between 1853 and 1861, during the height of Gold Rush, Fort Point was designed to stand sentry and protect against foreign attack on San Francisco Bay.

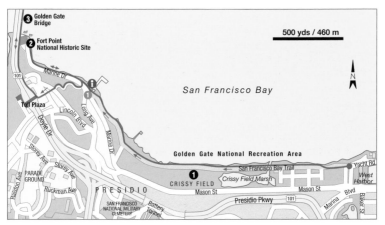

The bridge has six lanes of traffic and a sidewalk for pedestrians and cyclists

Highlights

A collection of exhibits and information relating to the fort's construction is found on the first floor. The floor above contains exhibits on the Fort Point lighthouses, African-American Buffalo Soldiers of the Civil War, and the roles of women in war. On the third floor, look for a photo exhibit of the Golden Gate Bridge's construction, for which Fort Point was the headquarters. Films also recount the construction of the fort and its history from 1776 through World War II.

Free 30-minute tours (call for times) leave from the front entrance, and special programs are offered, such as a demonstration of how a Napoleon 12-pounder cannon would be loaded and fired during a Civil War artillery drill.

GOLDEN GATE BRIDGE

Fort Point offers a unique vantage point from its location beneath the **Golden Gate Bridge ❸** (www.goldengate bridge.org). Work on the suspension bridge started on January 5, 1933, and was finished on May 27, 1937. More than 100,000 tons of steel were used, and its construction involved 25 million person-hours and the accidental death of 11 workers. It was the first bridge in the world to experiment with one-way toll collection.

When the city celebrated the Golden Gate's 50th anniversary in 1987, some 300,000 admirers made their way onto the bridge. It was the heaviest load the bridge had experienced in its history, and onlookers were shocked as the structure visibly sank beneath their weight.

Follow the signs to climb the bluffs to the bridge's toll plaza. The walk across the bridge is 3 miles (3km), and pedestrian access to the bridge is permitted during daylight hours only. (Note: there is no public transport stop to return to the city on the Marin side on weekdays, and pedestrians and cyclists share the same sidewalks.)

Misleading Name

Despite its name, the Golden Gate Bridge is actually painted a burned orange. The original plan was to paint the approach pylons on either side of the bridge gold, but no one ever took that idea seriously. The chief engineer, who thought most bridges, rather boringly, were painted gray, had suggested a silvery aluminum color, much like the color chosen for the 1936 Bay Bridge, though the final color is thought to be the responsibility of Irving Morrow, the bridge district's consulting architect, who was also responsible for the elegant Art Deco design. Known as "International Orange," the hue is a unique blend of orange and black paint that does look rather golden when the sun sets behind it.

Life Sciences Building

BERKELEY

Visit the liberal, diverse city and handsome university campus that became synonymous in the 1960s with the student Free Speech Movement, flower power, and student protests against the Vietnam War.

DISTANCE: 3 miles (5km)
TIME: A full day
START/END: Downtown Berkeley
POINTS TO NOTE: The distance noted above does not include detours to the Rose Garden, Lawrence Hall of Science, Botanical Gardens, or Tilden Park; the last three require a car or public transport for access. For lunch at Chez Panisse, call ahead for reservations.

Across the bay from San Francisco is the university town of Berkeley. Since the Free Speech Movement in 1964, it has been a hotbed of political activism. The university campus is a sprawling temple to education, full of earnest students and Nobel Prize-winning professors.

UNIVERSITY OF CALIFORNIA, BERKELEY CAMPUS

To reach the University Campus, take BART to the Downtown Berkeley station and then the Shattuck and Center streets exit. Turn right down Center and then left on Oxford Street to find the western entrance of the **University of California, Berkeley**. Enter the campus through the West Gate's semi-circular lawn and follow the long driveway onto campus. You will pass the 3-acre (1-hectare) **Valley Life Sciences Building** on the right, which is one of the largest academic facilities in the nation.

Campus libraries

Continuing east, you will pass the open-stack **Moffitt Library** and the adjacent **Free Speech Movement Café** ❶, on your left. Past the library, climb the staircase to the stunning Beaux Arts **Doe Library** ❶. Inside this main campus library, the lovely Morrison Library Reading Room to the right offers comfortable couches to sink into and rest; up the marble staircase (with hollows on each step worn down from years of student traffic) is the bright, airy, and cavernous North Reading Room, filled with long tables and canopied by an ornate coffered ceiling. In a nearby room hangs Emanuel Gottlieb Leutze's *Washington Rallying the Troops at Monmouth* (1854).

Berkeley graduates

Back outside, you can take a detour to visit to the North Berkeley Rose Garden off campus for gorgeous views. Cut north across Memorial Glade to the campus's North Gate, and wait for the 65 bus or walk north half of a mile on Euclid to Eunice Street. Just blocks off campus into the North Berkeley hills, the atmosphere changes dramatically: the noisy and hectic hubbub dies away, and winding streets grow wooded and peacefully residential.

To stay on campus, turn right from Doe Library and walk along grassy **Memorial Glade ❷**, a memorial to the alumni, faculty, and staff who served in World War II, and a favorite spot among students for sunbathing, napping, reading, and Frisbee-tossing.

Sather Tower

Turn right and walk towards the spindly **Sather Tower ❸**, better known as the Campanile. Built in 1914, the clock tower was modeled on the tower in Venice's Piazza San Marco, and named after a school benefactor, Jane K. Sather. The 61-bell carillon at the top of the tower sings out several times each day, and plays a dirge on the last day of classes before finals. Take the elevator (charge) to the top for wonderful views of the campus and bay. Then, you can choose to take a detour by bus to Berkeley Botanical Garden and Lawrence Hall of Science or walk southeast from Sather Tower, crossing the

Sather Tower

car-access road south of LeConte and Birge halls. North of LeConte Hall, look for parking spaces labeled 'NL' — these reserved spots are a choice bonus for the school's faculty members who have won the Nobel Prize. South of LeConte Hall, hop down the stairway, cross Strawberry Creek, and follow the path up around Faculty Glade. Pass Hertz Hall on the left and exit the campus onto Bancroft Way at College Avenue.

Berkeley Botanical Garden and Lawrence Hall of Science

To reach the Berkeley Botanical Garden or Lawrence Hall of Science up in Berkeley's hills, head north from Sather Tower to the Hearst Mining Circle just opposite Evans Hall, where the Hill Shuttle (the H Line) departs every half-hour (Mon–Fri 7.40am–6.10pm).

The **University of California Botanical Gardens ❹** (200 Centennial Drive; http://botanicalgarden.berkeley.edu; daily 9am–5pm, closed 1st Tue of month; charge, 1st Thur of month free) packs an amazing array of native California and exotic plant species into gardens high in the Berkeley hills. Another stop on the H Line is the **Lawrence Hall of Science ❺** (www.lhs.berkeley.edu; daily 10am–5pm; charge), which offers engaging hands-on exhibits related to maths and science. Kids also enjoy climbing on the giant whale outside, and everyone oohs and aahs over gorgeous views of San Francisco and the bay from the snack bar and parking lot. Return to campus and make your way back past the Sather Tower and on to Bancroft Way.

BERKELEY ART MUSEUM AND PACIFIC FILM ARCHIVE

Turn right on Bancroft Way for the **Berkeley Art Museum and Pacific Film Archive ❻** (No. 2626; www.bampfa.berkeley.edu; Wed–Sun 11am–5pm; charge except 1st Thur of the month). This collection of over 16,000 artworks includes works by Mark Rothko, Jackson Pollock, and Albert Bierstadt. Within the complex, the **Pacific Film Archive** offers daily screenings pulled from a pool of 14,000 movies, including international classics, Soviet silents, rare animation, and the largest collection of Japanese films outside of Japan.

TELEGRAPH AVENUE

Continue down Bancroft a few more blocks and turn left on **Telegraph Avenue ❼**, a counterculture landmark that bustles with students, panhandlers, and street vendors hawking everything from tie-dyed shirts to beaded and precious-metal jewelry. Telegraph is rife with eateries cheap enough for student budgets; try trusty **Top Dog ❷**. East of Telegraph and bordered by Haste Street and Dwight Way is **People's Park ❽**, the site of a legendary student-police confrontation in the late 1960s, now largely a hangout for the city's homeless population.

Sather Gate

Mural at the People's Park

SPROUL PLAZA AND SATHER GATE

Retrace your steps on Telegraph and cross Bancroft Way to re-enter the campus at **Sproul Plaza** ❾. This is where the Free Speech Movement kicked off in 1964; today, the busy plaza is frequently lined with student group tables and filled with demonstrators, alongside the odd-ball entertainer or evangelist.

Donated by Jane K. Sather in memory of her late husband Peder Sather, **Sather Gate** ❿ was once the end of Telegraph Avenue, a turning point for trolleys from Oakland, and the university's south-ern entrance. Now the landmark stands between Sproul Plaza and a bridge over Strawberry Creek.

Turn left at Sather Gate and walk downhill, keeping Strawberry Creek on your right. Look out for and then cross the wooden bridge with a tree growing out of the center, then bear left on the path ahead to exit the campus.

Cross Oxford onto Center, then turn right on Shattuck Avenue. If you are hungry, break at **Jupiter** ❸, or continue north on Shattuck to reach **Chez Panisse** ❹. Alternatively, turn right on Vine and then right on Walnut to find the heart of **Gourmet Ghetto** ⓫ and more tasty options.

Food and Drink

❶ FREE SPEECH MOVEMENT CAFÉ

Berkeley campus (at Moffitt Library); daily 8am–2am; $

Students line up between classes for coffee and black-bottom muffins at this animated campus café, then return for study-lunches over salads and panini. Getting a table can be tough because the students camp out for hours, but try to snag one outdoors.

❷ TOP DOG

2534 Durant Avenue; tel: 510-843-5967; www.topdoghotdogs.com; daily L and D; $

Open until 2am, Top Dog has been satisfying the post-party munchies for decades. Luckily, the *kielbasa*, bratwurst, and other specialty dogs are just as good earlier in the day.

❸ JUPITER

2181 Shattuck Avenue; tel: 510-843-8277; www.jupiterbeer.com; daily L and D; $$

A two-story brewpub with large tables, wood-fired pizzas, gourmet focaccia sandwiches, and great ambience. The fantastic brick-walled outdoor patio often hosts live jazz and folk music. Some 30 beers on tap, along with wine and pomegranate cider.

❹ CHEZ PANISSE

1517 Shattuck Avenue, Berkeley; tel: 510-548-5525; www.chezpanisse.com; Mon–Sat D only; $$$

The birthplace of California cuisine, founded by Alice Waters, who pioneered the use of local, seasonal ingredients. Courses are fixed by the chef, with two seatings each night. There is also a café that serves lunch.

DIRECTORY

Hand-picked hotels and restaurants to suit all budgets and tastes, organised by area, plus select nightlife listings, an alphabetical listing of practical information, and an overview of the best books and films to give you a flavor of the city.

Argonaut Hotel

ACCOMMODATIONS

Whatever your budget and traveling style, San Francisco offers a full spectrum of lodging options. At the most sophisticated (and expensive) end of the spectrum, the opulent Mandarin Oriental, Four Seasons, Ritz, and Taj offer every possible luxury. Equally refined, but with the added cachet of an impressive 100-plus-year pedigree, are San Francisco originals like the Fairmont on Nob Hill and the Palace Hotel on Market Street.

More moderately priced chains are also prevalent downtown, as well as in Fisherman's Wharf. Alternatively, try the small, amenities-rich boutique hotels with more definable personalities, such as literary, nautical, Tuscan, to name but a few. If you prefer cozy inns and bed and breakfasts, you'll find them in more residential areas further from the city center.

For true budget accommodations, there is a good selection of small hotels and no-frills lodgings. The dormitory-style Hostelling International San Francisco (www.sfhostels.com) has locations downtown near Union Square, in Fisherman's Wharf, and in Civic Center. All offer private and shared rooms, free daily breakfast and plenty of hosted activities, such as pizza and movie nights, walking tours, pub crawls, and more.

When making reservations at the larger hotels, ask about special packages and discounts, and check online booking sites to see if a better rate is available. Unless otherwise noted, all hotels are non-smoking.

Fisherman's Wharf

Argonaut Hotel
495 Jefferson Street; tel: 563-0800; www.argonauthotel.com; metro: F to Jones and Beach streets; cable-car: Powell–Hyde; $$$

The maritime-themed Argonaut sits just opposite the Hyde Street Pier. Rooms feature exposed red brick and nautical accents; suites offer sea views and tripod telescopes. Perks include a nightly wine hour and yoga mats in every room.

Best Western Plus Tuscan Inn
425 North Point Street; tel: 561-1100; www.tuscaninn.com; metro: F to Jefferson and Taylor streets; cable-car: Powell–Mason; $$

The Tuscan Inn is possibly the most pleasant of the many Fisherman's Wharf hotels, with charming guest rooms, a cozy "Living Room" with a nightly fireside

Price per night for a standard double room, excluding taxes and breakfast unless noted.
$$$$ = over $350
$$$ = $225–350
$$ = $150–225
$ = below $150

Hotel Monaco   *Hotel Bijou*

wine reception, and an on-site trattoria with traditional Tuscan favorites. Complimentary Wi-Fi throughout.

Hostelling International Fisherman's Wharf Hostel

240 Fort Mason; tel: 771-7277; www.sf hostels.com; bus: 30; $

Pleasant hostel located above the bay in a century-old army dispensary at Fort Mason, between the Marina and Fisherman's Wharf. Shared and private rooms in a variety of sizes, some of which are gender specific. Price includes free continental breakfast and access to self-service kitchen facilities. Complimentary Wi-Fi, plus computer terminals available for rent.

San Francisco Marriott Fisherman's Wharf

1250 Columbus Avenue; tel: 775-7555; www.marriott.com; $$

With easy access to the waterfront and North Beach (and just a short ride away from the Financial District), the Marriott is a convenient, all-in-one choice for families and business travelers, complete with a full-service business center, pet-friendly policies, a fitness center, and an on-site restaurant.

North Beach and Telegraph Hill

Hotel Boheme

444 Columbus Avenue; tel: 433-9111; www.hotelboheme.com; bus: 30, 39, 41, 45; $$

A throwback to the city's bohemian Beat era, this 15-room North Beach fixture pops with bright orange walls, checked bedspreads, and eclectic furniture and art. Front-desk staff happily assists with hired cars, dinner reservations, and tours. Wi-Fi is free.

San Remo Hotel

2237 Mason Street; tel: 776-8688 or 800-352-7366; www.sanremohotel.com; $

Built in 1906, this North Beach hotel was a boarding house for sailors, poets, and pensioners, then a speakeasy during Prohibition. Today it's a bargain getaway on a quiet street, with small, quaint rooms (no telephones or TVs), shared bathrooms, and free Wi-Fi. The rooftop penthouse is a treat.

Washington Square Inn

1660 Stockton Street; tel: 981-4220; www.wsisf.com; bus: 30, 39, 41; $$$

This European-style bed-and-breakfast offers a great location for an extended exploration of North Beach's legendary dining and nightlife scenes. Rates include breakfast for two, an evening welcome reception with wine and hors d'oeuvres, and wireless internet.

Union Square and Financial District

Andrews Hotel

624 Post Street; tel: 563-6877; www.andrews hotel.com; bus: 2, 3, 27, 38, 76; $

A bargain two blocks west of Union Square, this 1905 Victorian offers decid-

edly small rooms and baths, but makes up for it with historic charm, an intimate Italian restaurant, complimentary Continental breakfasts, evening wine receptions, and Wi-Fi.

Chancellor Hotel

433 Powell Street; tel: 362-2004; www.chancellorhotel.com; bus: 2, 3, 27, 38, 71; $$

Family-owned and managed since 1917, this charming, comfortably furnished hotel is a stone's throw from Union Square, and was once the tallest building in San Francisco. Backside rooms are quieter; rooms in the front offer views of the cable cars. Wireless internet is complimentary.

Clift Hotel

495 Geary Street; tel: 775-4700; www.clift hotel.com; bus: 2, 4, 27, 38, 76; $$$

Redesigned by Philippe Starck, this historic hotel is now a fusion of old-world elegance and modern style. Rooms feel light and fresh, decorated in a creamy palette with lavender accents. For less serenity and more buzz, the legendary Redwood Room is just downstairs.

Four Seasons

757 Market Street; tel: 633-3000; www.fourseasons.com; metro: all lines to Montgomery; cable-car: Powell–Hyde, Powell–Mason; $$$$

The Four Seasons knows how to cater to its sophisticated and fairly exclusive clientele, boasting an ultra-convenient downtown location, an in-house tech-center, high-end stores, and a two-story health club with an indoor pool and Jacuzzi.

Golden Gate Hotel

775 Bush Street; tel: 392-3702; www.goldengatehotel.com; $$

A vintage elevator connects the 4 floors of this lovingly maintained 25-room Edwardian inn with highly rated service. Rooms feature traditional decor and antique furniture are some have claw-foot bathtubs. A continental breakfast is included and there is free Wi-Fi.

Grand Hyatt

345 Stockton Street; tel: 398-1234 www.hyatt.com; $$$

High style and high-tech features attract business travelers to this newly renovated tower hovering over Union Square. Sumptuous facilities include an on-site restaurant, coffee bar, and gym, as well as conference and event spaces.

Handlery Union Square Hotel

351 Geary Street; tel: 781-7800; http://sf.handlery.com; bus: 2, 4, 27, 38, 71; $$

This historic, family-owned hotel is a good family choice, with an outdoor heated pool, babysitting services, same-day laundry service, a business center, pet-friendly policies, and morning and evening room service. Larger club rooms in an adjacent building offer fresh decor, dressing areas, and newspapers.

Hilton and Tower San Francisco

333 O'Farrell Street; tel: 771-1400 or 800-445-8667; www.hilton.com; $$

With 1,685 rooms on the edge of Union Square, this is one of the largest hotels in the city, complete with a pool, exercise room, and five restaurants. The popular Urban Tavern restaurant serves gastro-pub cuisine.

Hostelling International Downtown Hostel

312 Mason Street; tel: 788-5604; www.sfhostels.com; bus: 38, 38L; $

This large hostel has both shared rooms (maximum 4 beds per room) and private rooms, some with ensuite bathrooms. Price includes a free continental breakfast and access to self-service kitchen facilities. Complimentary Wi-Fi, plus computer terminals available for rent.

Hotel Bijou

111 Mason Street; tel: 771-1200 or 800-771-1022; www.hotelbijou.com; $$

Black-and-white images of old cinema marquees cover the walls of this 65-room hotel for cinephiles, where each room spotlights a different film integral to California cinema – from *The Birds* to *Dirty Harry*, *American Graffiti* to *Joy Luck Club*. Nightly viewings in the mini-theater with vintage cinema seating and free popcorn are a quirky bonus. $

Hotel des Arts

447 Bush Street; tel: 956-3232 or 800-956-4322; www.sfhoteldesarts.com; $

Near Chinatown, this bastion of hipness promises an unforgettable and inexpensive stay. Each of the modest "painted" rooms is a unique canvas created by a local artist. The hotel is a gallery of underground urban art; there is a French brasserie on the street level.

Hotel Diva

440 Geary Street; tel: 885-0200 or 800-553-1900; www.hoteldiva.com; $$$

Steely modern decor, artist-designed lounges, a 24-hour fitness center, and Starbucks coffee shop located just off the lobby are some of the draws of this boutique hotel in the Theater District.

Hotel Metropolis

25 Mason Street; tel: 775-4600 or 877-775-4600; www.hotelmetropolis.com; $$

Simple rooms are decorated in earth tones or water-themed blues in this ten-story eco-friendly hotel with a "four elements" theme. Complimentary tea and coffee service and free Wi-Fi.

Hotel Monaco

501 Geary Street; tel: 292-0100; www.monaco-sf.com; bus: 2, 3, 27, 38, 76; $$$

This renovated Beaux Arts building evokes glamorous from the get-go, with hand-painted ceiling domes and grand Art Nouveau murals in golden-hued common areas. Rooms boldly play with colors and patterns, and amenities include whirlpool tubs in most suites, yoga accessories, and 24-hour room

Hotel Triton

service. Rates include morning coffee and evening wine receptions. Pets are allowed for no extra charge.

Hotel Nikko

222 Mason Street; tel: 394-1111; www.hotelnikkosf.com; metro: all lines to Powell; cable-car: Powell–Mason, Powell–Hyde; $$$

Close to Union Square, this elegant Japanese offers comfortable, well-equipped rooms, a heated indoor poor, steam room, sauna, and 24-hour fitness center. The on-site ANZU restaurant serves Californian cuisine with Asian influences and also features a sushi bar.

Hotel Rex

562 Sutter Street; tel: 433-4434; www.jdvhospitality.com; cable-car: Powell–Hyde, Powell–Mason; $

Inspired by the San Francisco literary salons of the 1920s and 30s, the Rex is a treat for bibliophiles. Complimentary Wi-Fi, morning coffee and newspaper, and an evening wine hour are offered, and you can enjoy live jazz on Fridays in the library bar.

Hotel Triton

342 Grant Street; tel: 394-0500; www.hoteltriton.com; bus: 2, 30, 45, 76; $$

Across from Chinatown Gate, the eco-friendly Triton is a green hotel pioneer, employing a sophisticated recycling program, energy-efficient systems, and other environmentally-conscious practices. The lobby's wild designs and mod furniture are amusing, though the bedrooms are tiny.

Mandarin Oriental

222 Sansome Street; tel: 800-622-0404; www.mandarinoriental.com; metro: all lines to Montgomery; cable-car: California Street; $$$$

This luxury hotel offers jaw-dropping views and the most decadent service. Binoculars are provided in each room, and some of the rooms have glass bathtubs situated near the windows.

Omni San Francisco Hotel

500 California Street; tel: 677-9494; www.omnihotels.com; cable-car: California Street; $$$

Built as a bank in 1926, the refined Omni welcomes guests off California Street cable-cars into a lobby adorned with Italian marble, rich fabrics and Austrian crystal chandeliers. The 362 guest rooms exude classic sophistication and comfort, with marble bathrooms and 9ft (2.7m) -high ceilings with crown moldings. Downstairs is Bob's Steak & Chop House.

Powell Hotel

28 Cyril Magnin; tel: 398-3200; www.thepowellhotel.com; $$

Ornate 20ft (6m) ceilings and marble floors greet guests in the grand lobby, and with the clang of the cable car and the carnival of Market Street below, the small but affordable rooms ensure a

Well-staffed reception desk

Doorman at the Ritz–Carlton

classic San Francisco experience in the middle of the action. The deluxe rooms and suites are a good option for families or those who need a little more space.

Prescott Hotel

545 Post Street; tel: 563-0303; www.prescotthotel.com; $$

Rooms decorated in calming neutrals set a timeless scene; but complimentary Wi-Fi, yoga mats in every room, and a friendly hosted wine hour are all very modern. In-room spa treatments featuring organic beauty products are available.

Renaissance Parc 55

55 Cyril Magnin; tel: 392-8000 or 800-595-0507; www.parc55hotel.com; $$

This four-diamond, luxury hotel in a convenient downtown location has a 24-hour fitness center, mounds of comfy pillows, and great views from the upper floors. Dining options include an on-site Thai restaurant and the Cityhouse bar and steakhouse.

Ritz-Carlton

600 Stockton Street; tel: 296-7465; www.ritzcarlton.com; cable-car: California Street; $$$$

Once a giant neoclassical corporate headquarters, this luxury landmark hotel lives up to expectations. It boasts 336 rooms and facilities include an indoor spa with gym, swimming pool, whirlpool, and sauna, and an award-winning French restaurant on the premises.

Serrano

405 Taylor Street; tel: 885-2500; www.serranohotel.com; bus: 27, 38; cable-car: Powell–Hyde, Powell–Mason; $$

This Spanish-Moroccan-styled hotel in the heart of the Theater District features lavish lobby furnishings and 236 guest rooms decked out in dark woods, saffron yellow walls, and red-and-white striped curtains. A 24-hour fitness center is on site, as is the Jasper's Corner Tap and Kitchen.

Sir Francis Drake

450 Powell Street; tel: 392-7755; www.sirfrancisdrake.com; bus: 2, 3, 27, 38, 74; $$$

This 1928 landmark is known for its doormen decked out in Beefeater costumes, and its spectacular views. Rooms are styled as if from an English country home, which is perfect for the traveling Anglophile. There's also a small fitness room, nightclub.

Taj Campton Place

340 Stockton Street; tel: 781-5555; www.taj hotels.com; bus: 2, 4, 30, 45, 76; cable-car: Powell–Mason, Hyde–Mason; $$$$

Elegant, and intimate, this refined hotel is perfect for the sophisticated and discreet traveler, offering excellent service, top-notch amenities, a consistently highly rated restaurant, and a spa.

The Touchstone

480 Geary Street; tel: 771-1600; https://thetouchstone.com; $

The marble floor entrance at the Westin St Francis

This 42-room budget option is small all around – including the rooms and elevator – but at two blocks west of Union Square, it's extremely convenient. Free wireless internet is available in rooms, and the business center offers free internet and printing services.

Westin St Francis

335 Powell Street; tel: 397-7000; www.westinstfrancis.com; cable-car: Powell–Hyde, Powell–Mason; $$$

A San Francisco institution since 1903, this Union Square hotel is rich in history and elegance. Meeting beneath the hand-carved grandfather clock in the lobby has long been a favorite rendezvous for locals. If the historic aspects interest you, reserve a room in the original building: the baths are small and rooms rather dark, but they are furnished with handsome reproductions and chandeliers. Chef Michael Mina's acclaimed Bourbon Steak restaurant is on site.

SoMa and Civic Center

Adagio Hotel

550 Geary Street; tel: 775-5000; www.thehoteladagio.com; bus: 27, 38; $$$

The Adagio is comfortable and chic, with Aveda bath products and a room decor scheme that pairs greys, apple green, and deep burgundy to a sophisticated effect. Ask for a room with a view.

Harbor Court Hotel

165 Steuart Street; tel: 882-1300; www.harborcourthotel.com; metro: F to Don Chee Way and Steuart Street; $$$

Elegant boutique hotel in a 1907 building that offers comfortable rooms, luxury amenities, bay views, and complimentary access to the state-of-the-art fitness center next door.

Hostelling International City Center Hostel

685 Ellis Street; tel: 474-5721; www.sfhostels.com; bus: 38, 38L; $

Centrally located budget option, with both shared rooms, with 4 or 5 beds, and private rooms. Price includes a free continental breakfast and access to self-service kitchen facilities. Complimentary Wi-Fi, plus computer terminals available for rent.

Hotel Palomar

12 4th Street; tel: 866-373-4941; www.hotelpalomar-sf.com; $$$

Enjoy cheerful, casually elegant rooms, a complimentary wine tasting each night, and close proximity to all the Union Square shopping action. Corner King rooms offer good views of the street cars on Market Street.

Hotel Vitale

8 Mission Street; tel: 278-3700; www.hotelvitale.com; metro: all lines to Embarcadero; $$$

This waterfront hotel features earthy, subdued tones and with 180-degree views of the Embarcadero, Bay Bridge,

Fairmont Hotel and Tower　　　　　　　　　　*Luxury hotel room*

and Ferry Building. Complimentary yoga classes are available in the morning, along with private soaking tubs, and secret gardens. Treatments also available at Spa Vitale.

Hotel Zetta

55 5th Street; tel: 543-8555; www.viceroy hotelgroup.com; $$$

Sleek and hi-tech in a playful way, the new downtown Hotel Zetta is a fun take on ultra-modern luxury. Facilities include a games room and brasserie-style restaurant.

InterContinental San Francisco

888 Howard Street; tel: 888-811-4273; www.intercontinentalsanfrancisco.com; bus: 14, 27; $$$

This blue-glass tower is sexy, technologically sophisticated, and earned the highest certification for green practices. Guest rooms have floor-to-ceiling windows and plenty of amenities. A luxurious spa, Bar 888, and Luce restaurant are on the premises.

Mosser

54 4th Street; tel: 986-4400; www.the mosser.com; metro: all lines to Powell; $–$$

An ornate stained-glass window in the lobby, antique phone booths, and an incredibly slow elevator are quirky reminders of this hotel's past, but the good linens, latest gadgets, prime SoMa location, and good rates make it an affordable choice for young sophisticates.

Palace Hotel

2 New Montgomery Street; tel: 512-1111; www.sfpalace.com; metro: all lines to Montgomery; $$$$

This opulent historical landmark just south of Market is home to the magnificent Garden Court Restaurant. Enjoy cocktails under the Maxfield Parrish mural in the Pied Piper bar.

W Hotel

181 3rd Street; tel: 777-5300; www.whotels.com; bus: 9, 14, 30, 45, 76; $$$$

Vibrantly modern and trendy, the high-design W offers both an urban refuge for travelers (check out the Bliss spa menu) and a lively nightlife scene for those who want to mingle.

Nob Hill

Fairmont Hotel and Tower

950 Mason Street; tel: 772-5013; www.fairmont.com; cable-car: California Street; $$$

A favorite set location for film-makers, the opulent Fairmont on the crest of Nob Hill has been accommodating guests since 1907. Today, the spacious rooms and impeccable service attract a loyal clientele. The penthouse suite takes up the entire eighth floor, and has an Art Deco motif that will leave you breathless.

Huntington Hotel

1075 California Street; tel: 474-5400; www.huntingtonhotel.com; cable-car:

The ornate exterior of the InterContinental Mark Hopkins

California; $$$$

Plush, elegant, and still family owned, the Huntington is one of the city's small, luxury gems. Each room and suite is uniquely decorated, the service is flawless, and it's home to one of the city's best spas. For the best views, book a room above the 8th floor.

InterContinental Mark Hopkins

1 Nob Hill; tel: 392-3434; www.ichotelsgroup.com/intercontinental; cable-car: California Street; $$$

Situated where Mark Hopkins's mansion once stood, this hotel offers luxury rooms, grand views in all directions, and an atmosphere of quiet refinement. The "Top of the Mark" restaurant and bar remains a must-do on any trip to San Francisco, while the rooms never fail to satisfy.

Petite Auberge

863 Bush Street; tel: 928-6000; www.petitieaubergesf.com; cable-car: Powell–Hyde, Powell–Mason; $

A small, cozy, French-style inn that offers a pretty parlor for afternoon wine and a gourmet breakfast included in the price. A good value option near Union Square.

Renaissance Stanford Court

905 California Street; tel: 989-3500; www.mariott.com; cable-car: California Street; $$$

A fine renovation here set the standard for San Francisco grand hotel revivals. Enjoy great views and the quintessen-tial San Francisco sound of cable-cars ding-dinging outside your window.

White Swan Inn

845 Bush Street; tel: 775-1755; www.whiteswaninnsf.com; cable-car: Powell–Hyde, Powell–Mason; $$

The romantic rooms and suites at this cozy, English-style bed-and-breakfast feature characterful fireplaces and comfortable sitting areas. Enjoy gourmet breakfast buffets, afternoon tea with home-baked cookies, and evening wine and hors d'oeuvres served fireside in the parlor. An English-style bed and breakfast inn, the White Swan has gas fireplaces in all 26 rooms – quaintly atmospheric and useful in chilly and fog-bound San Francisco.

Central Neighborhoods

Chateau Tivoli

1057 Steiner Street; tel: 776-5462; www.chateautivoli.com; bus: 21, 22; $

A plush Victorian bed-and-breakfast inn on picturesque Alamo Square brimming with antiques and curios. Some of the 22 attractive rooms feature fireplaces and Jacuzzis.

Hotel Del Sol

3100 Webster Street; tel: 921-5520; www.jdvhospitality.com; bus: 22, 43, 76; $

Once an ordinary motel, the Del Sol's radical makeover splashed color on walls, fabrics, and mosaic tiles decorating tabletops and walkways. Comfortable rooms surround a heated swimming

Renaissance Stanford Court

The street outside the Renaissance Stanford Court

pool, small lawn, and hammock. Suites are available.

Hotel Majestic

1500 Sutter Street; tel: 441-1100; www.the hotelmajestic.com; bus: 2, 3, 4, 38; $$

An old-world atmosphere prevails at the Majestic, which was constructed in 1902 and claims to be the oldest still-operating hotel in the city. Rooms are cozy and festooned with swags and draperies. Good-value special rates.

Haight-Ashbury and Golden Gate Park

Inn 1890

1890 Page Street; tel: 386-0486; bus: 7, 33, 37, 43, 71; $

This beautiful bed-and-breakfast built in 1890 is located just one block from Golden Gate Park and one block from colorful Haight Street. Some of the 18 rooms feature fireplaces.

Red Victorian

1665 Haight Street; tel: 864-1978; www.redvic.com $

The Red Victorian is perfect for the budget traveler. Located in the heart of the Haight- Ashbury district, this small hotel is friendly, with each room reflecting a different theme, like the "Flower Child Room" or the "Playground," all commemorating the Summer of Love in Golden Gate Park. The Red Vic is also home to the Peace Arts gallery, gift shop, and café, which aims to inspire conversations about peace.

Stanyan Park Hotel

750 Stanyan Street; tel: 751-1000; www.stanyanpark.com; bus: 7, 33, 43, 66, 71; $

Elegant and affordable, this early-20th-century boutique hotel is steps from Golden Gate Park and Haight Street. Suites are large and ideal for families; a continental breakfast is included.

The Mission and Castro

24 Henry Guesthouse

24 Henry Street; tel: 864-5686; www.24henry.com; metro: K, L, M, T to Church; $

This late-1800s house in the Castro has been refurbished and turned into a guesthouse with a parlor and five bedrooms. The owners also have another Victorian guesthouse, Village House, just five blocks away.

Inn on Castro

321 Castro Street; tel: 861-0321; http://innoncastro.com; $

The perks of this humble 8-room B&B? A full breakfast, fresh flowers, a back patio, and an unbeatable location for enjoying the Castro.

Parker Guesthouse

520 Church Street; tel: 621-3222; www.parkerguestouse.com; metro: J to Church Street and 18th Street; $

A relaxed and welcoming Castro guesthouse with 21 rooms (two with shared bathrooms), a garden, steam room, and terrycloth robes for every guest.

An original takeout hatch

RESTAURANTS

San Francisco is internationally known as an incredibly rich destination for foodies. From ground-breaking California and exciting fusion cuisines to adventurous ethnic dishes, there are thousands of restaurants competing for your taste buds – those that don't make the grade soon fall from notice, and those that do are on everyone's lips. Some districts are known for particular fare (the Mission for *taquerías*, North Beach for Italian, and Chinese on the Inner Richmond's Clement Street, but nearly all neighborhoods offer a wide variety of cuisines for every meal of the day.

Fisherman's Wharf

Albona

545 Francisco Street; tel: 441-1040; www.albonarestaurant.com; Wed–Mon D only; cable car: Powell-Mason; bus: 30, 39; $$$

An intimate and "homey" Istrian restaurant serving Northern Italian dishes influenced by the flavors of Central and Eastern Europe, such as homemade

Price guide for a three-course meal and half a bottle of house wine for one person:
$$$$ = over $100
$$$ = $50–100
$$ = 25–50
$ = below $25

ravioli stuffed with three cheeses, pine nuts, golden raisins, and fresh ground nutmeg, and braised rabbit with onions, honey, and juniper berries.

Alioto's

8 Fisherman's Wharf; tel: 673-0183; www.aliotos.com; daily L and D; cable car: Powell Mason; metro: F; bus: 47; $$

In San Francisco, the Alioto name stands for politics, feuds, family, and fine food. For generations, this famous family-owned establishment has ruled the Wharf with fresh, local seafood and Sicilian dishes.

Blue Mermaid

471 Jefferson Street; tel: 771-2222; www.bluemermaidsf.com; daily B, L, and D, metro: F to Jones and Beach streets; cable-car: Powell–Hyde; $$$

Housed in the historic Argonaut Hotel, chowder dominates this menu. The sampler option is a great way to try a selection of the different recipes on offer. The nautical interior adds to the experience, as do the sourdough soup bowls.

Gary Danko

800 North Point Street; tel: 749-2060; www.garydanko.com D daily; $$$$

Shuttered to the outside, epicurean pleasures are the only focus here. The menu is neatly divided between a three-

Fort Mason restaurant   *Spicy ribs*

and five-course tasting menu that places diners completely in the hands of the world-renowned chef. It is quite possibly the best food San Francisco has to offer.

In 'N Out Burger

333 Jefferson Street; tel: 800-786-1000; www.in-n-out.com; daily L and D; metro: F; bus: 30; 47; $

Founded in 1948, In 'N Out is possibly the most loved fast food chain in California. In old-fashioned diner digs, this Fisherman's outpost is an easy stop for a simple – and good – burger, fries, and milkshake.

McCormick and Kuleto's

900 North Point Street, Ghirardelli Square; tel: 929-1730; www.mccormickandschmicks.com; daily L and D; cable-car: Powell–Hyde; bus: 19, 47; $$$

From the relaxed, redwood-paneled dining room, you can enjoy waterfront views of Alcatraz, Marin and historic ships as you choose from a huge variety of fresh, imaginative seafood dishes and American favorites.

Scoma's

Pier 47; tel: 771-4383; www.scomas.com; daily L and D; metro: F to Jefferson and Taylor streets; $$$

For a glimpse of the working man's wharf, dine right on the pier at this old-school Italian spot that has served seafood, pasta, and its acclaimed clam chowder for 50 years.

North Beach

Firenze by Night

1429 Stockton Street; tel: 392-8485; http://firenzebynight.ypguides.net; daily D; bus: 30, 41, 45; $$

The house specializes in traditional Northern Italian fare – pillowy-soft gnocchi, tender calamari, and pappardelle *pasta Toscana* with rabbit – but the long menu pleases all tastes. Treat yourself to a house-made limoncello with dessert.

L'Osteria del Forno

519 Columbus Ave; tel: 982-1124; Mon, Wed–Sun L and D; www.losteriadelforno. com; bus: 30, 41, 45; $$ (cash and travelers checks only)

For casual but satisfying Italian food, including antipasti, thin-crusted pizzas, and a fine roast pork loin, head to this tiny gem that captures the spirit of North Beach.

Molinari Delicatessen

373 Columbus Ave; tel: 421-2337; www.molinarisalame.com; bus: 30, 41, 45; $

This classic Italian deli is a North Beach institution. In addition to deli sandwiches, you'll find imported cheese, cured meats, and canned goods, and Molinari's own selection of sausage salamis and raviolis made in Hunters Point.

North Beach Restaurant

1512 Stockton Street; tel: 392-1700; www.northbeachrestaurant.com; daily L and D; bus: 30, 41, 45; $$$

Gourmet scallops

A warm, relaxing spot serving hearty Tuscan cuisine. The menu features home-made pastas, home-cured prosciutto and classic Italian seafood dishes, accompanied by a dizzyingly comprehensive wine list.

O'Reilly's

622 Green Street; tel: 989-6222; www.sforeillys.com; daily B, L, and D; bus: 30, 41, 45; $

This re-creation of an Irish pub is a cozy place for a hearty brunch or dinner, either in the cool, stoneworker interior, or on the pleasant sidewalk tables. Try the Guinness-battered fish and chips or the choice burgers.

Peña Pacha Mama

1630 Powell Street; tel: 646-0018; http://penapachamama.com; Wed–Sun D only; bus: 30, 41, 45; $$

Bolivian hospitality, robust organic flavors, traditional tapas like plantains and *yucca frita*, and live traditional music most nights make dining here an unforgettable experience. Raw, gluten-free and vegan selections available.

Chinatown

Bix

56 Gold Street; tel: 433-6300; www.bixrestaurant.com; daily D; bus: 10, 12, 41; $$$

Swank digs, upscale Californian munchies, and live jazz are served at this stylish, two-story supper club with plush banquettes and cozy booths. Enjoy a pre-dinner cocktail or order something special from their extensive wine list.

Hunan Homes

622 Jackson Street; tel: 982-2844; http://hunanhome.ypguides.net; daily L and D; bus: 10, 12, 41; $$

Service is brusque at this popular restaurant, but the massive menu doesn't disappoint. Local favorites include the orange peel chicken, pot stickers, and sweet and sour soup.

House of Nanking

919 Kearny Street; tel: 421-1429; daily L and D; bus: 10, 12, 41; $

Grungy and crowded, the reason for the line at nearly all hours is because this popular spot is a neighborhood favorite. What it lacks in atmosphere it makes up for in deliciousness. Take the advice of the no-nonsense owners and staff on what to order, and avoid weekends.

Financial District

Barbacco

220 California Street; tel: 955-1919; www.barbaccosf.com; Mon–Fri L and D, Sat D only; cable car: California; bus: 1; $$$

There's always a lively buzz at this modern Italian trattoria in the Financial District. Exposed brick walls, low lights, and small communal tables set a casually cool vibe, while the Italian small plates are delicious: bruschetta, house-cured salumi, Sicilian meatballs with raisins and pinenuts, and amazing fried brus-

Racks of wine

Top marks for presentation

sels sprouts. Its mature big sister next door, Perbacco, is more formal.

Cotogna

490 Pacific Avenue; tel: 775-8508; www.cotognasf.com; Mon–Sat L and D; Sun D only; bus: 10, 12; $$

Next door to its fine dining sister restaurant, Quince, Cotogna is a more casual (and less expensive) alternative. The rustic Italian menu changes daily, including spit-roasted or grilled meats and fish, wood-oven pizzas and house-made pastas.

Kokkari

200 Jackson Street; tel: 981-0983; www.kokkari.com; Mon–Fri L and D, Sat D only; bus: 10, 12; $$$$

The best place in the city for sophisticated Greek food, this inviting, upscale taverna lures dinners to the border of North Beach and the Financial District to feast (below its beamed ceilings and by its massive fireplace) on feta cheese filo pies, spiced and grilled lamb skewers, and of course walnut and honey baklava with vanilla-praline ice cream.

Sam's Grill

374 Bush Street; tel: 421-0594; www.belden-place.com/samsgrill; Mon–Fri L and D; bus: 30; 45; $$$

Relive the days of three-Martini business lunches at this downtown grill, still going strong after 125 years. Dine on American cuisine in the high-ceilinged dining room or private booths.

A comprehensive menu includes classic dishes from Bay shrimp cocktail and clam chowder to Caesar salad and New York steak.

Slanted Door

1 Ferry Building #3; tel: 861-8032; www.slanteddoor.com; daily L and D; metro: F to Embarcadero and Ferry Building; cable-car: California; $$$

Wholesome, flavorful, and modern Vietnamese food at one of the city's premier restaurants. The menu features a mouth-watering selection of carefully sourced meat, fish and poultry dishes, plus vegetable sides and mains. At afternoon tea, sip hard-to-find Chinese varieties. Reservations required.

Tadich Grill

240 California Street; tel: 391-1849; Mon–Sat L and D; cable-car: California; bus: 1; $$$

Around in various incarnations since the Gold Rush, this institution offers old-school San Francisco ambience – from the original mahogany bar to the waiters as crusty as the sourdough – and a menu of classics including lobster Newburg, crab Louis, and sand dabs.

Gott's Roadside

1 Ferry Building #6; tel: 866-328-3663; www.gotts.com; daily L and D; metro: F to the Embarcadero and Ferry Building; cable-car: California; $

Sit on picnic benches outside at this stylish burger joint which uses seasonal

Hot dog sign

ingredients. Dig into high-end diner fare with a gourmet flourish, from California beef burgers, to thick milkshakes and sweet-potato fries.

Wayfare Tavern

558 Sacramento Street; tel: 772-9060; www.wayfaretavern.com; daily L and D; bus: 1; $$$

The pre-meal popovers are so delicious at Tyler Florence's upscale tavern that it's hard not to have three. But restrain yourself, because the menu of American comfort food (with a turn-of-the-20th-century twist) includes gems like deviled eggs, organic fried chicken, and Scharffen Berger chocolate cream pie... and you'll want every last bite!

Union Square and Tenderloin

Le Colonial

20 Cosmo Place; tel: 931-3600; http://lecolonialsf.com; daily D; bus: 2, 3, 27, 76; $$$

Upscale French-Vietnamese fare amid gentle, swirling ceiling fans and leafy palm trees transports diners to another world. A great respite, with creative cocktails and appetizers.

Fleur de Lys

777 Sutter Street; tel: 673-7779; www.hubertkeller.com/restaurants/fleur-de-lys; daily D; bus: 2, 3, 27, 76; $$$$

The city's premier French restaurant provides elegant and romantic formal fine dining, superior service, and an exhaustive wine list.

Osha Thai

696 Geary Street; tel: 278-9991; www.oshathai.com; daily L and D bus: 2, 3, 27; $

There are five other outposts of this popular Thai restaurant (including one on 2nd Street and one in Cow Hollow), but this one stays open til 2am, making it a great pit-stop between bar-hopping downtown.

Sears Fine Food

439 Powell Street; tel: 986-0700; www.searsfinefood.com; daily L and D; cable car: Powell-Hyde and Powell Mason; bus: 2, 3; $$

At this old-school San Francisco institution (since 1938!) you can have sourdough French toast and Swedish pancakes for breakfast, club sandwiches and Bay shrimp Louie for lunch, and prime rib or San Francisco *cioppino* (a fish stew) for dinner.

Shalimar

532 Jones Street; tel: 928-0333; www.shalimarsf.com; daily L and D; bus: 27, 38; $

One of the city's best Indian restaurants, this simple spot serves Indian and Pakistani food in a noisy, but relaxed atmosphere. No alcohol; cash only.

Urban Tavern

333 O'Farrell Street; tel: 923-4400; www.urbantavernsf.com; L, D daily $$$

A good option for a pre- or post-theater rendezvous, this gastropub in the Hilton

Exquisite dessert   *Freshly grilled steak*

offers a chic, loft-like atmosphere and a menu with lamb sliders, strip steak, stuffed trout, and a decadent mac and cheese.

South of Market

Alexander's Steakhouse

448 Brannan Street; tel: 495-1111; www.alexanderssteakhouse.com; D daily; bus: 30, 45, 47; $$$$

Sometimes nothing will satisfy like a good steak. You can quell that craving with classic cuts like Porterhouse, New York, and T-bone from grain-fed Angus beef in the handsome glass-and-brick dining room.

Boulevard

1 Mission Street; tel: 543-6084; www.boulevardrestaurant.com; Mon–Fri L and D; Sat–Sun D only; bus: 41; $$$

A great special-occasion destination, this Embarcadero landmark delivers exceptional American regional food in an elegant Belle-Epoque inspired setting. The wood-oven specialties, like the pork prime rib chop with crispy bacon and sauerkraut dumplings, are standouts. Reservations essential.

Le Charm

315 5th Street; tel: 546-6128; www.lecharm.com; Tue–Sat D only; bus: 12, 27, 30, 45; $$

Ratatouille, *escargots*, duck confit, crème brûlée, French onion soup: French food's greatest hits share this comfortable, unpretentious stage.

Town Hall

342 Howard Street; tel: 908-3900; www.townhallsf.com; Mon–Fri L, Sat–Sun L and D; bus: 12, 30, 45, 76; $$$

Regional American classics such as buttermilk fried chicken, cornmeal-fried oysters, smoked andouille jambalaya are served in a stylishly remodeled historic building.

Tres Agaves

130 Townsend Street; 227-0500; www.tressf.com; daily L and D; $$

Excellent Mexican food pairs perfectly with the voluminous tequila-heavy drinks menu. Adventurous diners are encouraged to explore the diversity of agave's nectar by the knowledgeable staff. Tasting flights are on offer – but stay away from the habanera-infused tequila.

Yank Sing

49 Stevenson Street; tel: 541-4949; www.yanksing.com; Mon–Fri 11am–3pm, Sat–Sun 10am–4pm; metro: all lines to Montgomery; $$

A sure-fire dim sum pleaser, with fresh ingredients in a sparkling clean interior and particularly tasty dumplings.

Civic Center and Hayes Valley

Absinthe Brasserie and Bar

398 Hayes Street; tel: 551-1590; www.absinthe.com; Tue–Sun L and D; bus: 21, 47, 49; $$$

Ideal a romantic dinner before the symphony, ballet or opera (or a refresher

Vegetarian sushi

after exploring Civic Center and Hayes Valley), this upscale brasserie serves American-influenced French and Northern Italian fare in a casually romantic atmosphere – think leather banquettes, antique mirrors, and period art. The soft garlic pretzels are a local favorite.

Ananda Fuara

1298 Market Street; tel: 621-1994; www.anandafuara.com; Mon–Tue and Thur–Sat B, L and D, Wed B and L only; metro: all lines to Civic Center; $

Ananda Fuara (meaning "Fountain of Delight") is a sure bet for inexpensive, delicious, and varied vegetarian and vegan picks, from curry wraps to mushroom ravioli and vegan chocolate cake.

Espetus

1686 Market Street; tel: 552-8792; www.espetus.com; daily L and D; metro: F, J, K, L, M to Van Ness; $$$ (prix fixe)

Eat until you burst at this Brazilian steakhouse in the South American *churrascaría* style. Copious skewered meats are brought to your table and carved on the spot.

Suppenküche

525 Laguna Street; tel: 252-9289; www.suppenkuche.com; Br Sun, D daily; bus: 21; $$

One of only a few German restaurants in the city, updated German classics – spaetzle, schnitzel, fried potato pancakes, and hearty soups – are served to diners sitting family style on long spartan benches. Around 20 beers (mostly German) on tap.

Zuni Café

1658 Market Street; tel: 552-2522; www.zunicafe.com; Tue–Sun L and D; metro: all lines to Van Ness; $$

Make reservations and elbow past the crowded copper bar for the best roasted chicken and bread salad (for two) imaginable. The daily changing menu is inspired by traditional Italian and French recipes. Floor-to-ceiling windows, sidewalk tables, and an upstairs loft all add to Zuni's allure. Closed Monday.

Nob Hill and Russian Hill

Nick's Crispy Tacos

1500 Broadway Street; tel: 409-8226; www.nickscrispytaco.com; daily L and D; $

Locals rave about the cheap, delicious tacos at this ultra-relaxed joint. No one wastes time with the burritos, just order your tacos "Nick's Way" and you will not be disappointed.

Nob Hill Grille

969 Hyde Street; tel: 474-5985; www.nobhillgrille.com; daily D, Sat–Sun brunch; $$

Homey cuisine is served in a stylish but laid-back atmosphere at this cozy neighborhood spot. Classic meat dishes like roasted chicken, pot pie, and burgers prevail at this former diner turned grown-up grille.

Chinese stir-fry   *Beautiful presentation*

Zarzuela

2000 Hyde Street; tel: 346-0800; Mon–Sat L and D; cable-car: Powell–Hyde; bus: 41, 45; $$

Bring hungry friends to this cheerful Spanish restaurant atop Russian Hill and share tapas, paella, and sangria as cable-cars roll by.

Swan Oyster Depot

1517 Polk Street; tel: 673-1101; Mon–Sat 10.30am–5.30pm; bus: 1; $

This seafood counter has been around since 1912, and crowds line up for a seat. Seafood salads and cocktails, lobster, Dungeness crab, and oysters.

Marina

A16

2355 Chestnut Street; tel: 771-2216; www.a16sf.com; Wed–Fri L, and D daily; bus: 28, 20, 43; $$

With an open kitchen up front and a crowded bar, lively A16 dishes up wood-fired Neapolitan pizzas and other rustic fare inspired by southern Italy, particularly Campania.

Betelnut

2030 Union Street; tel: 929-8855; www.betelnutrestaurant.com; daily L and D; bus: 41, 45; $$

A Pan-Asian bar-restaurant specializing in dumplings and noodle bowls with bold, exciting flavors. Large mugs of beer make a good accompaniment to some of the spicier dishes.

La Boulange

1909 Union Street; tel: 440-4450; www.laboulangebakery.com; daily B and L; bus: 41, 45; $

With a dozen outposts in San Francisco (the address above is for the Marina district), this French bakery and café was recently acquired by Starbucks. It's a go-to for locals when they're craving croissants and decadent French pastries, open-faced sandwiches, or a simple brunch.

Central Neighborhoods

Cha Cha Cha

1801 Haight St, 2327 Mission Street; tel: 386-7670, 824-1502; www.cha3.com; daily L and D; $$

If you're in the mood for a boisterous atmosphere, tasty tapas, and pitchers of sangria, Cha Cha Cha's outposts in the Haight and Mission districts are the place to go. No reservations.

DOSA on Fillmore

1700 Fillmore Street; tel: 441-3672; www.dosasf.com; bus: 2, 3, 22; $$

In a lofty and chic 200-seat space, Dosa serves up authentic Southern Indian regional cuisine with an innovative spin. Dishes like Tamil lamb curry, mango prawns, and Dahi Vada (lentil dumplings) can be paired with international wines or a gin-based "spice-driven" cocktail.

Kiss

1700 Laguna Street; 474-2866; Tue–Sat D

Mission District restaurant

only; bus: 2, 3, 38; $$$
This bite-sized spot is perhaps the city's best Japanese restaurant, with outstanding sushi and sake, a simple and elegant atmosphere, and great service.

Fresca
2114 Fillmore St, 3945 24th St; www.frescasf.com; Mon–Tue D only; Wed–Sun L and D; bus: 1, 22; $$
In a lively dining room with an open kitchen, hungry couples and groups dig into nouveau Peruvian cuisine, including delicious fresh ceviche and savory *lomo saltado*.

NOPA
560 Divisadero Street; tel: 864-8643; www.nopasf.com; daily D only; bus: 21, 24; $$$
Eclectic, wood-fired cuisine is the specialty here, from pork chops with grilled peaches to spicy fennel sausage flatbreads and tasty fried fish. Open until 1am.

Haight-Ashbury and Golden Gate Park

Park Chow
1240 9th Avenue; tel: 665-9912; www.chowfoodbar.com; daily B, L, and D; metro: N to 9th and Irving; bus: 44, 71; $
South of Golden Gate Park, this casual, family-friendly eatery serves simple comfort food – pastas, sandwiches, salads and pizzas – either downstairs by the fireplace or upstairs on the patio (don't worry, there are heat lamps!)

The Mission and Castro

Bissap Baobab
2323 Mission Street; tel: 826-9287; www.bissapbaobab.com; Tue–Sun D only; bus: 14, 33, 49; $$
A funky international spot with a diverse clientele, serving West African fare and refreshing, potent cocktails. Standout dishes include spinach pastelle pastry, *mafe* with tofu in a peanut sauce, and oniony chicken *dibi* with couscous.

Delfina
3621 18th Street; tel: 552-4055; www.delfinasf.com; D daily; bus: 14, 49; $$$
Ultra-fresh seasonal ingredients go into the creative Italian fare at this crowded Mission hotspot. For a less expensive, but equally delicious option, try Pizzeria Delfina next door (tel: 437-6800; www.pizzeriadelfina.com).

Frances
3870 17th Street; tel: 621-3870; www.frances-sf.com; D daily; metro: F, K, M, L; bus: 4, 33, 35, 37; $$$
This relaxed Castro eatery is a firm favourite with local foodies. Chef-owner Melissa Perello's daily changing menu of modern-Cal cuisine offers dishes like Sonoma duck breast with butter-bean ragout, and caramelized scallops with toasted faro and wild mushrooms. Reservations recommended.

La Taquería
2889 Mission Street; tel: 285-7117; daily L

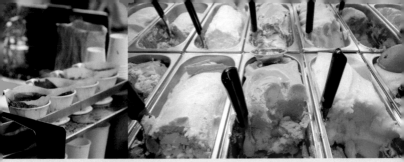

Fresh coffee   *Delicious ice cream flavors*

and D; BART: 24th Street; bus: 12, 14, 49; $

The epitome of the casual Mission district *taquerías*, this immensely popular spot is a perfect place to grab some *carnitas* tacos.

Little Star Pizza

400 Valencia Street (also 846 Divisadero Street); tel: 551-7827; www.littlestarpizza.com; BART: 16th Street; bus: 14, 33, 49; $

Local hipsters flock to Little Star for their deep-dish pizza with Chicago-style crust – it's no wonder President Obama loves the recipe. Decor is simple, with exposed brick walls and wooden tables and chairs, but it hardly matters because everyone's focused on the pizza! The "Little Star" (spinach blended with ricotta and feta, mushrooms, onions, garlic) is a local fave. No reservations.

Puerto Alegre

546 Valencia Street; tel: 255-8201; daily L and D; BART: 16th Street; $

Boisterous groups descend on this Mexican table-service restaurant to get well fed and a little tipsy from pitchers of Margaritas.

Range

842 Valencia Street; tel: 282-8283; www.rangesf.com; daily D only; BART: 24th Street; $$

This warm, inviting space serves savory contemporary Californian cuisine; the short but excellent menu includes dishes such as roasted chicken with an artichoke, toasted almond, and bacon bread salad.

Rosamunde's Sausage Grill

2832 Mission Street; tel: 970-9015; www.rosamundesausagegrill.com; daily L and D; bus: 14, 49; $

If you're feeling peckish in the Mission or the Lower Haight districts the perfect snack awaits you at Rosamunde's. This local favorite has over a dozen types of grilled sausage to choose from (smoked pork, bacon-wrapped beef, duck and figs) and a hefty beer selection to pair with it.

Outer Neighborhoods

Aziza

5800 Geary Boulevard; tel: 752-2222; www.aziza-sf.com; daily D; bus: 38; $$$

Hike to the Outer Richmond and be rewarded with upscale, modern versions of Moroccan dishes. The menu is influenced by California cuisine's emphasis on organic, locally produced ingredients.

Sutro's at the Cliff House

1090 Point Lobos; tel: 386-3330; www.cliffhouse.com; daily L and D; metro: N to Ocean Beach; $$$

Incredible views of the ocean, Golden Gate, and Marin Headlands make this smart, well-designed Ocean Beach restaurant a truly desirable option for seasonal California cuisine.

The bright lights of the bar

NIGHTLIFE

San Francisco provides an enticing array of cultural diversions. Operatic arias and symphonic melodies waft through concert halls, jazz bands sizzle in intimate clubs, and hot rock, pop, and alternative bands jam on small stages and in spacious arenas alike. Theatrical flavors and fancy footwork run the gamut from classical to cutting-edge, and cinephiles enjoy much-loved art-house theaters and film festivals. The thirsty and hard-partying sets are not disappointed either, with sounds and spirits for all tastes.

Bars and Clubs

15 Romolo
15 Romolo Place; tel: 398-1359; www.15romolo.com; Mon–Fri 5pm–2am, Sat–Sun 11.30am–2am
Tucked up on an alley between Broadway strip clubs, this is one of the best picks in North Beach for a good cocktail. Weekends are always busy, and the jukebox always playing.

21st Amendment
563 2nd Street, tel: 369-0900; www.21st-amendment.com; Mon–Sat 11.30am–midnight; Sun 10am–midnight
With a small beer garden and a lofted, industrial interior, there is plenty of space for beer and baseball fans to enjoy the charms of this famed SoMa brewery. It also serves excellent pub food made from seasonal and local ingredients.

The Alembic
1725 Haight St; tel: 666-0822; www.alembicbar.com; Mon–Fri 4pm–2am, Sat–Sun noon–2am
If you're craving a superlative cocktail near Haight-Ashbury, sidle up to The Alembic's bar, where mixology is an art form.

Amelie
1754 Polk Street; tel: 292-6916; www.ameliesf.com; daily 6pm–2am
This crimson-walled wine bar at the foot of Nob Hill features a French-heavy menu, well-dressed clientele, and an inviting atmosphere.

Bar Agricole
355 11th Street; tel: 355-9400; www.baragricole.com; Sun–Thur 5pm–10pm, Fri–Sat 5pm–11pm
Sip on small-batch spirits in a modern industrial space — or the heated garden patio, weather permitting.

Blackbird
2124 Market Street; tel: 503-0630; www.blackbirdbar.com; Mon–Fri 3pm–2am, Sat–Sun 2pm–2am
Looking to sip craft cocktails with a chic crowd in the Castro? This is your spot.

The cocktail hour

Celebrations at the bar

Bourbon and Branch

501 Jones Street; tel: 346-1735;
www.bourbonandbranch.com; daily
5pm–3am

The secret's out about this speakeasy where masterfully mixed libations are poured. The telltale "Anti-Prohibition League" gives away the location, and passwords "books" or "cigar" get you into the "Library"; reserve to access the main bar. For the ultimate in secrecy, Wilson and Wilson is the speakeasy within the speakway.

Dalva

3121 16th Street; tel: www.dalvasf.com;
daily 4pm–2am

Chill in the low-key front room, or head to "the Hideout" back-room lounge for a custom cocktail and top-shelf liquours.

Edinburgh Castle

950 Geary Street; tel: 885-4074;
www.castlenews.com; daily 5pm–2am

This Scottish-run Tenderloin pub offers quiz nights on Tuesdays, DJs Friday and Saturday nights, pool and darts, a fantastic Scotch inventory, plus fish and chips delivery.

Elbo Room

647 Valencia Street; tel: 552-7788;
www.elboroom.com; daily 5pm–2am

Flirt over pinpall and pool at this longtime Mission standby, or head upstairs for music, including Afrolicious's Thursday parties and reggae Sunday. The daily happy hour stretches from 5–9pm.

El Rio

3158 Mission Street; tel: 282-3325;
www.elriosf.com; Mon–Thur 5pm–2am,
Fri–Sun 1pm–2am

Diverse crowds flock to this friendly, funky bar for popular "Salsa Sundays" on the patio.

The End Up

401 6th Street; tel: 646-0999;
www.theendup.com; Thur 10pm–4am, Fri
11pm–Sat 1pm, Sat 10pm–Mon 4am

A diverse, gay-friendly crowd dances and carouses until dawn and beyond in this South of Market club.

Hemlock Tavern

1131 Polk Street; tel: 923-0923;
www.hemlocktavern.com;
daily 4pm–2am

Underground rock bands light up the back; hipster punk rockers snack on warm peanuts up front. Bonus: heated outdoor smoking lounge.

La Trappe

800 Greenwich St; tel: 440-8727;
http://latrappecafe.com; Tue–Wed 6pm–
midnight, Thur–Sat 5pm–midnight

Kick off a night in North Beach with burgers and Belgian brews at this lively underground bar and restaurant.

Local Edition

691 Market Street, tel: 795-1375;
http://localeditionsf.com; Mon–Fri
5pm–2am, Sat 7pm–2am

A nondescript entrance on Market

Chinatown bar

Street leads you down to the subterranean depths of the historical Hearst building, now a swanky cocktail bar that pays homage to its past with vintage paper presses and newspaper clippings.

Matrix Fillmore

3138 Fillmore Street; tel: 563-4180;
www.matrixfillmore.com; Mon–Thur
8pm–2am, Fri–Sun 6pm–2am

A fixture of the young Marina singles scene that is awash with designer-jean-clad beauties.

Mezzanine

444 Jessie Street; tel: 625-8880;
www.mezzaninesf.com; hours vary

Dance to beats from international and hot new talents at this mega-club located in South of Market.

Noc Noc

557 Haight Street; tel: 861-5811;
www.nocnocs.com; daily 5pm–2am

An easygoing, fun-loving crowd fills this funky Lower Haight dive with Flintstones c.1986 decor.

Press Club

20 Yerba Buena Lane; tel: 744-5000;
www.pressclubsf.com; Mon–Thur
4pm–11pm, Fri–Sun 2pm–2am

A sophisticated underground wine-tasting bar and lounge just off Market Street, Press Club is popular with post-work crowds treating clients or letting off steam with co-workers.

Rye

688 Geary Street; tel: 474-4448;
www.ryesf.com

For a good cocktail near Union Square, the dark and moody Rye is a solid bet. One side is a lounge (with an outdoor smoking cage), the other has the bar and pool table.

Rickhouse

246 Kearny Street; tel: 398-2827;
www.rickhousebar.com; Mon 5pm–2am,
Tue–Fri 3pm–2am, Sat 6pm–2am

Financial District workers packs this narrow bar with artisanal cocktails after work on weekday, but it's busy at weekends too, with live music every Saturday.

Ruby Skye

420 Mason Street; tel: 693-0777;
www.rubyskye.com; Thur–Sat 8pm–4am

Ready to get your dance on? Major DJs pack this massive Union Square club. Dress to impress.

Smuggler's Cove

650 Gough Street; tel: 869-1900;
smugglerscovesf.com;
daily 5pm–1.15am

The tiki bar to out-umbrella all tiki bars, with pirate and nautical themed decor, punch bowls with giant straws, and an indoor waterfall, not to mention a daunting menu of 75 cocktails and some 400 rums. Don't like sweet drinks? Try "Three Dots and a Dash" — Morse code for "victory."

LGBT-friendly bar in Castro   *Catching up over a beer*

Top of the Mark
1 Nob Hill; tel: 616-6916;
www.topofthemark.com; Mon–Thur
4.30–11.30pm, Fri–Sat until 12.30am, Sun
10am–10pm
Sip martinis (there are 100 to choose
from), listen to the piano play, and enjoy
the gorgeous views of the city and the
Golden Gate Bridge from this elegant
lookout on Nob Hill.

Toronado
547 Haight Street; tel: 863-2276;
www.toronado.com; daily 11.30am–2am
A high temple for craft beer devotees in
San Francisco, with dozens of obscure
beers, and Rosamunde's sausages
available from next door.

Zeitgeist
199 Valencia Street; tel: 255-7505; daily
9am–2am
Day and night, tattooed hipsters soak
up sun on the large, bench-filled patio,
consuming burgers, brews, and Bloody
Marys.

Cabaret
Asia SF
201 9th Street; tel: 255-2742;
www.asiasf.com; Tue–Sun D only
"Gender illusionists" serve Cal-Asian
cuisine and saucy entertainment every
hour on the red runway bar.

Beach Blanket Babylon
Club Fugazi, 678 Green Street; tel: 421-
4222; www.beachblanketbabylon.com;

performances Wed–Thur 8pm, Fri–Sat
6.30pm and 9.30pm, Sun 2pm and 5pm
A campy pop-culture spoof and legendary experience. Adults only except for
Sunday matinees. Arrive early.

Teatro ZinZanni
Pier 29; tel: 438-2668; http://love.zinzanni.
org; performances Wed–Sat 6.55pm, Sun
5.55pm (also Tue 6.55pm in Dec)
Over-the-top cabaret, circus, and spec-
tacle are served during an eclectic five-
course dinner. Arrive early.

Classical Music
Louise M. Davies Symphony Hall
201 Van Ness Avenue; tel: 864-6000;
www.sfsymphony.org
This elegant hall houses the acclaimed
San Francisco Symphony Orchestra
from September to July.

War Memorial Opera House
301 Van Ness Avenue; tel: 864-3330;
www.sfopera.com
The glamorous Beaux Arts War Memorial Opera House fills from September
to November and May to July with those
keen to hear the San Francisco Opera
Company perform.

Other Venues
Outside the two main venues above, the
city's major companies perform at the
Yerba Buena Center for the Arts (YBCA)
and the Herbst Theater in the War
Memorial Veterans Building. The Old
First Presbyterian Church (1751 Sacra-

Live jazz at Lou's Pier 47 Blues Club

mento Street; tel: 474-1608; www.old firstconcerts.org) runs a chamber and recital repertoire.

Comedy

Cobb's Comedy Club
915 Columbus Avenue;
tel: 928-4320; www.cobbscomedy club.com
The biggest names in television play this, the city's largest comedy room.

Punch Line
444 Battery Street; tel: 397-7573;
www.punchlinecomedyclub.com
The best national stand-up comics regularly headline this small club, Dave Chapelle, Dave Attell, Greg Proops, and David Cross among them.

The Purple Onion at Kells
530 Jackson Street; tel: 730-2359;
http://purpleonionatkells.com
This historic, intimate nightclub offers comedy and music.

Contemporary Music

Bimbo's 365 Club
1025 Columbus Avenue; tel: 474-0365;
www.bimbos365club.com
Rock, jazz, and more swing this swank 1930s-throwback nightclub, which also has comedy and burlesque on occasion.

Fillmore Auditorium
1805 Geary Boulevard; tel: 346-6000;
www.thefillmore.com

Major headliners play this legendary venue where Bill Graham launched his empire in the 1960s.

Great American Music Hall
859 O'Farrell Street; tel: 885-0750;
www.musichallsf.com
A former Barbary Coast bordello complete with ornate balconies now attracts international rock, folk, and blues acts.

The Independent
628 Divisadero Street; tel: 771-1421;
www.theindependentsf.com
Popular for live rock, punk, indie pop, folk, hip-hop, and more.

Slim's
333 11th Street; tel: 255-0333;
www.slims-sf.com
Packed SoMa spot with a mix of blues, R&B, and alternative touring acts.

Dance

The San Francisco Ballet (tel: 865-2000; www.sfballet.org) performs traditional full-length ballets and contemporary pieces from February through April at the War Memorial Opera House, and an ever-popular winter *Nutcracker* production. Alonzo King's LINES Ballet (tel: 863-3040; www.linesballet.org) is a top-notch globetrotting contemporary ballet company that performs locally at the Yerba Buena Center for the Arts (YBCA). Another contemporary company is ODC Dance (tel: 863-6606; www.odcdance.

Jazz bar in Chinatown

org), known nationally for its artistic innovation.

Jazz and Blues

Biscuits and Blues

401 Mason Street; tel: 292-2583; www.biscuitsandblues.com; Tue–Thur 8–11.30pm, Fri–Sat 3.30–11.30pm

A nationally well-respected blues club that teams Southern cuisine with live blues and a relaxed atmosphere.

Boom Boom Room

1601 Fillmore Street; tel: 673-8000; www.boomboomblues.com; Tue–Sat 8pm

Blues, boogie, groove, and soul keep this funky little joint hopping.

Yoshi's

1330 Fillmore Street; tel: 655-5600; www.yoshis.com; shows: Mon–Sat 8pm and 10pm, Sun 7pm and 9pm, restaurant: daily D only

Jazz giants jam at this outpost of Oakland's famed Jack London Square club.

Theater

TIX Bay Area (tel: 433-7827; www.tixbayarea.com) in Union Square sells half-price performance-day tickets from 11am. Other third-party ticket agents (which will add a booking fee) include TickCo (tel: 800-279-4444; www.tickco.com) and City Box Office (tel: 392-4400; www.cityboxoffice.com). The city's fringe theater venues include: Exit Theatre (tel: 673-3847; www.sffringe.org), Intersection for the Arts (tel: 626-2787; www.theintersection.org), The Marsh (tel: 800-838-3006; www.themarsh.org), the New Conservatory Theatre Center (tel: 861-8972; www.nctcsf.org), and Project Artaud Theatre (tel: 626-4370; www.artaud.org).

American Conservatory

415 Geary Street; tel: 749-2228; www.act-sf.org

A Tony Award-winning regional theater that delivers solid classical and contemporary fare.

Curran Theater

445 Geary Street; tel: 551-2000; www.shnsf.com

Broadway favorites and try-outs are staged in this elegant, historic theater.

Magic Theatre

Fort Mason Center, Building D, at Marina Boulevard and Buchannan Street; tel: 441-8822; www.magictheatre.org

Dedicated to new works, this stage has premièred an impressive list of plays.

Orpheum Theatre

1192 Market Street; tel: 551-2000; www.shnsf.com

Large-scale Broadway productions fill this grand, historical landmark.

Chinatown and the Transamerica Pyramid

A–Z

A

Age restrictions

You must be over 21 years of age to be able to drink legally in San Francisco. The minimum legal age for smoking is 18 years old. Expect to have to show I.D. to buy alcohol in bars, clubs, and restaurants.

C

Children

One of the great things about traveling with children in San Francisco is that many of the city's attractions are suitable for people of all ages. A stroll across the Golden Gate Bridge, exploring the markets of Chinatown, cresting a hill aboard a cable-car, or zigzagging down legendary Lombard Street are all crowd-pleasers for young and old alike. San Francisco is a very kid-friendly city with an abundance of state-of-the-art playgrounds, restaurants that offer children's menus (and often crayons), bathrooms equipped with changing tables for babies, and lots of wide open spaces for running around in. Most hotels allow children to stay in parents' rooms at no additional charge (though there is usually an age limit for this) and will provide a rollaway bed or portable crib as needed.

Climate

San Francisco weather can change significantly from hour to hour and between neighborhoods. Springs are pleasantly warm and sunny (average high in April 63°F/17°C; low 50°F/10°C), while summers can be overcast and typified by fog (average high in July 66°F/19°C; low 54°F/12°C). Come September and October, the summer chill is replaced with beautifully mild, sunny days (average high in September 70°F/21°C; low 56°F/14°C). Rainstorms (no snow) appear in December and January, though crisp, sunny days offer breaks from the damp and dreary ones (average high in January 56°F/14°C; low 46°F/8°C).

Clothing

Plan for variable weather and bring clothes that can be layered, as well as comfortable walking shoes: the city's hills are hard to climb in high heels. A raincoat and sturdy umbrella are vital for winter months, when windy rainstorms are common. The city's casual, come-as-you-are vibe means jeans, T-shirts, and tennis shoes are ubiquitous on streets and in many restaurants and entertainment venues. However, fancier eateries and nightclubs usually warrant something a bit smarter.

Mural on Ross Street   *Catching the ferry*

Crime and safety

As a major city, San Francisco does see some crime, and travelers should exercise good common sense, avoiding seedy neighborhoods and being cautious about walking around alone and at night. Avoid parks after dark. Neighborhoods with less safe reputations include the Tenderloin, Civic Center, Western Addition, the Lower Haight, the Mission south of 24th Street, South of Market above 5th Street, and Bayview districts.

Customs

Adult visitors staying longer than 72 hours may bring the following into the country duty-free: 1 liter of wine or liquor; 100 cigars (non-Cuban), or 3lbs of tobacco, or 200 cigarettes; and gifts valued under $100.

Pay careful attention to restrictions on bringing food into the US, as violating them results in heavy fines. Agricultural items – including anything with meats, fruits, vegetables, plants, soil, and products made from animal or plant materials – are not permissible. As a general rule, bakery items, certain cheeses, condiments, vinegars, oils, packaged spices, honey, coffee, and tea are admissible. Visitors may also arrive and depart with up to $10,000 currency without needing to declare it. For the most up-to-date information on what you can bring with you, refer to the U.S. Customs and Border Protection website (www.cbp.gov).

D

Disabled travelers

The city's topography presents obvious challenges to those who have mobility problems, but San Francisco is relatively disabled-friendly. The San Francisco Travel Association maintains a TDD/TYY information line (392-0328) and offers a free accessibility guide (www.sanfrancisco.travel/accessibility/San-Francisco-Access-Guide.html). For guidance on public transportation, request the Muni Access Guide from Muni Accessible Services Programs (701-4485 or TTY 701-4730). Handicapped parking zones are clearly marked throughout San Francisco with signage and blue curbs; obtain a temporary permit at the Department of Motor Vehicles at 1377 Fell Street (bring along your state-of-origin permit/plaque with photo ID; fee $6).

Societies that can provide useful information include **MossRehab** (tel: 800-2255-6677; www.mossresource net.org) and the Society for Accessible Travel & Hospitality (SATH; tel: 212-447-7284; www.sath.org).

E

Electricity

Electricity in the U.S. is 110 Volts, 60 Hertz A.C. Flat-blade, two-pronged plugs are typical, though some points have three-pronged sockets. Most for-

Chinese New Year parade

eign appliances need a transformer and/or plug adapter.

Embassies/consulates

Australia: tel: 644-3620; www.dfat. gov.au.
Canada: tel: 834-3180; http://can-am. gc.ca/san-francisco/.
Ireland: tel: 392-4214; http://www. consulateofirelandsanfrancisco.org.
France: tel: 397-4330; www.consul france-sanfrancisco.org
Germany: tel: 775-1061; www.germany. info/SanFrancisco.
New Zealand: tel: 650-342-4443; www.nzembassy.com.
South Africa: tel: 202-232-4400; www. saembassy.org.
U.K.: tel: 617-1300;
www.gov.uk/government/world/organ isations/british-consulate-general-san-francisco.
Details for other embassies and consulates can be found by a simple Google search.

Emergency numbers

For ambulance, fire, or police, dial 911; if you need to call from a public phone, no coins needed.

Environmental issues

With an extensive recycling program, a bike-riding population, and countless campaigns to "green" the city by planting trees and native species on its rooftops and public spaces, San Francisco has rightly developed a reputa-

tion for being an eco-friendly city. But as much as it tries, it is also a densely populated metropolitan area that carries the inevitable environmental concerns, ranging from air quality to water shortages. San Francisco's greatest threat lies just below the surface in the network of seismic faults that occasionally jolt the city and can cost lives and millions of dollars' worth of damage.

F

Festivals

January
San Francisco Sketchfest. National headliners, local favorites and up-and-coming groups all converge for a month-long spree of sketch, improv, stand-up and alternative comedy.
Dr Martin Luther King Jr.'s Birthday Celebrations. Events across town.

February
Chinese New Year Parade. With floats, firecrackers, and a fantastic lion orchestrated by 100 costumed dancers, this annual celebration of the lunar new year has become one of the largest events of its kind outside Asia. www.chinese parade.com.
Noise Pop. An indie music festival going strong for over 20 years.

March
St Patrick's Day Parade. A full day of celebration at Civic Center (and bars

The annual pride celebration and parade

around town, especially in the Financial District) and one of the longest-running parades in the U.S.

April

Cherry Blossom Festival. Two weekends of Japanese art, music, and food. www.nccbf.org.

San Francisco International Film Festival. www.sfiff.org.

May

Bay to Breakers. San Francisco's 12km Bay to Breakers is the oldest consecutively run annual footrace in the world, held since 1912. Participants don outrageous costumes and wind their way through the city, from the Embarcadero to Ocean Beach. www.baytobreakers.com.

Carnaval. Hispanic Mission district comes alive with floats, dancers, and Latino music. www.carnavalsf.com.

San Francisco International Beer Festival. www.sfbeerfest.com

June

Escape From Alcatraz Triathalon. www.escapefromalcatraztriathlon.com

Haight Street Fair. One of the city's biggest street fairs, with 200+ booths offering foods and crafts, and live music all day. www.haightashburystreetfair.org.

North Beach Festival. The city's oldest street fair. www.sresproductions.com

San Francisco Pride Celebration and Parade. A weekend of events including a huge Sunday parade. www.sfpride.org.

San Francisco Silent Film Festival. www.silentfilm.org.

Stern Grove Festival. Classical, jazz, world music, and picnics (June–Aug). www.sterngrove.org.

July

Fourth of July Waterfront Festival. Independence Day celebrations feature live music and firework displays over the bay. www.fishermanswharf.org.

Fillmore Jazz Festival. www.fillmorejazzfestival.com.

Jewish Film Festival. www.sfjff.org.

San Francisco Shakespeare Festival. Free Shakespeare in the Park and programs for youngsters, from July through September. www.sfshakes.org.

August

Nihonmachi Street Fair. A celebration of the Bay Area's Asian- and Pacific-American communities. www.nihonmachistreetfair.org.

Outside Lands Festival. A huge 3-day music festival in Golden Gate Park. www.sfoutsidelands.com.

September

Comedy Day. Free stand-up in Golden Gate Park. www.comedyday.com.

Free Opera in the Park. "Greatest hits" performed by the San Francisco Opera in Golden Gate Park and live performances simulcast in AT&T Park. Free.

Using the Wi-Fi connection at a local café

San Francisco Fringe Festival. Independent theater, performance art, and comedy held in various venues. www.sffringe.org.

Folsom Street Fair. San Francisco's R-rated BDSM and leather subculture street festival. www.folsomstreetfair.com

October

Fleet Week. Fisherman's Wharf welcomes the U.S. Navy. Highlights include the Blue Angels airshow. www.fleetweek.us

Hardly Strictly Bluegrass Festival. Some of the biggest names in bluegrass, country, and rockabilly perform free for three days in Golden Gate Park. www.hardlystrictlybluegrass.com.

Litquake. A 9-day literary event for booklovers, filled with readings, panel-discussions, and literary bar crawls. www.litquake.org

November

Christmas Tree Lighting Ceremonies. The city lights up in Union Square on the Saturday after Thanksgiving.

Día de los Muertos. The Mexican Day of the Dead is celebrated with drummers, altars, and dancing skeletons. www.dayofthedeadsf.org.

December

Festival of Lights. The lighting of a Hanukkah menorah in Union Square.

New Year's Eve. City-wide celebration with live music and fireworks.

G

Gay and lesbian

San Francisco is internationally known as one of the world's most welcoming places for gays and lesbians, and this accepting attitude prevails in all neighborhoods. The most predominantly gay district is the Castro. The best source for information are two free weeklies: the *Bay Area Reporter* (www.ebar.com) and the *Bay Area Times* (www.sfbaytimes.com). it's also worth consulting www.sanfrancisco.travel/lgbt/. The Center (1800 Market Street; tel: 865-5555; www.sfcenter.org; Mon–Thur noon–10pm, Fri noon–6pm, Sat 9am–6pm; free) is a vital nexus for the LGBT community, and has an information desk and library, plus web access, bulletin boards, and a café.

Guided tours

San Francisco City Guides (www.sfcityguides.org) offers a range of free, volunteer-led tours, covering both neighbourhood overviews and specialty topics such as Alfred Hitchock, architecture, wall murals, the 1906 earthquake, and theatre. Foot! (www.foottours.com), Wok Wiz Chinatown Tour (www.wokwiz.com), and Cruisin' the Castro (www.cruisinthecastro.com) also offer interesting tours at reasonable prices. In addition, several bus tour companies also offer daily tours

Pharmacy sign

in and around the city; see www.san-francisco.travel for a complete list.

For guided tours outside of the Bay Area, Green Tortoise (tel: 800-8678-6473; www.greentortoise.com) is an adventurous option; each trip makes frequent stops at national parks or other points of interest, and their buses have communal areas that convert to reclined sleeping quarters at night. The San Francisco headquarters also house the Green Tortoise hostel.

H

Health

Drugstores (pharmacies)

Some medicines that are available over the counter in your home country may require a prescription in the U.S. There are branches of the useful 24-hour Walgreens drugstore chain (www.walgreens.com) at 498 Castro Street (tel: 861-3136) and 3201 Divisadero Street (tel: 931-6417). Additional Walgreens and Rite Aid (www.riteaid.com) branches are open late into the evening.

Insurance and hospitals

Healthcare is private and can be very expensive, especially if you need to be hospitalized. Foreign visitors should always ensure that they have full medical insurance covering their stay before traveling to the U.S. The following hospitals have 24-hour emergency rooms:

California Pacific Medical Center
Castro Street at Duboce Avenue; tel: 600-6000; www.cpmc.org; Metro: N to Duboce.

Saint Francis Memorial Hospital
900 Hyde Street; tel: 353-6300; www.saintfrancismemorial.org; bus: 1, 2, 19, 27.

San Francisco General Hospital
1001 Potrero Avenue; tel: 206-8000; www.sfdph.org; bus: 9, 10, 33, 48, 90.

UCSF Medical Center
505 Parnassus Avenue; tel: 476-1000; www.ucsfhealth.org; Metro: N to UCSF.

I

Internet

Many cafés have Wi-Fi hotspots, although some establishments impose time limits on usage. If you're looking for not only free internet access but also a computer to use, public library branches are your best bet. Contact the San Francisco Public Library for information (tel: 557-4400; http://sfpl.org).

L

Lost property

Lost property is handled by the San Francisco police department (http://sf-police.org), and found items are held at the Property Clerk's Room for 120 days. To report lost items, phone a local police station, or from Mon–Fri 9am–4pm, contact the Property Clerk, tel: 415-553-1392.

Tipping is expected in bars and restaurants

M

Media

The largest regional newspaper is the *San Francisco Chronicle* (www.sfgate. com); its Sunday "Pink Pages" list art, music, and entertainment events. Free alternative weeklies are found in newspaper boxes, cafés, and bars. The four main weeklies are the *San Francisco Bay Guardian* (www.sfbg.com), *SF Weekly* (www.sfweekly.com), San Francisco Bay Times (www.sfbaytimes. com), and *Bay Area Reporter* (www. ebar.com). The last two are gay- and lesbian-oriented, and most easily found in the Castro. The city's magazines include *San Francisco Magazine* (www. modernluxury.com/sanfrancisco) and 7x7 (www.7x7.com).

Money

Currency

The dollar ($) is divided into 100 cents (¢). The coins are the penny (1¢), nickel (5¢), dime (10¢), quarter (25¢), and the less common half-dollar (50¢) and $1 coins. The banknotes are the $1, $5, $10, $20, $50, and $100 bills.

Banks and currency exchange

Bank hours are generally Monday to Friday, from about 9am to 5pm. Some open on Saturday mornings. It's best to change foreign currency at airports, major banks downtown, or American Express offices.

ATMs

ATMs are at banks, some stores, and bars, and charge varying usage fees: check also with your bank at home. Debit card use on purchases at major grocery and drugstores allows you to get cash back.

Credit cards

Credit cards are accepted at most restaurants, hotels, and stores.

Traveler's checks

With the popularity of ATMs, credit cards, and debit cards, traveler's checks are increasingly less common. However, banks and some stores, restaurants, and hotels do accept traveler's checks in U.S. dollars. If yours are in foreign denominations, they must first be changed to dollars. Un-exchanged checks should be kept in your hotel safe. Record the checks' serial numbers in a separate place to facilitate refunds of lost or stolen checks.

P

Police

The emergency police number is 911 (no coins needed). The non-emergency number for the police is 553-0123.

Postal services

Post offices open at 8–9am and close at 5–6pm, Monday through Friday; the post office in the Macy's department store on Union Square (tel: 956-0131)

Police badge

San Francisco is a great city for walking

is also open on Sunday. Use the Civic Center post office for general-delivery mail (poste restante).

U.S. Postal Service
Tel: 800-275-8777; www.usps.com.

Civic Center Post Office
101 Hyde Street; tel: 563-7284; Mon–Fri 9am–5pm.

Public holidays

The U.S. has shifted most public holidays to the Monday closest to the actual dates, thereby creating a number of three-day weekends. Most banks, post offices, government buildings, and some large businesses are closed on the following national holidays:

New Year's Day January 1

Martin Luther King Jr. Day 3rd Monday in January

President's Day 3rd Monday in February

Memorial Day Last Monday in May

Independence Day July 4

Labor Day 1st Monday in September

Columbus Day 2nd Monday in October

Veterans Day November 11

Thanksgiving Day 4th Thursday in November

Christmas Day December 25

Smoking

Be careful where you light up in San Francisco: smoking laws are strict, and smoking is banned in many public places such as offices, shops, restau-rants, and bars. Many hotels are completely non-smoking. The minimum legal age for smoking is 18 years old.

T

Taxes

In San Francisco, an 8.75 percent sales tax is added to the price of all goods and services; in surrounding cities, the sales tax ranges from 8–9 percent. Hotels charge a 14 percent tax that generally will not be included in quoted rates.

Telephones

Local calls are inexpensive; long-distance calls are decidedly not. Public phones accept coins and calling cards. The San Francisco area code is 415, which you only need to dial from outside the city; the country code is 1. Toll-free numbers begin 1-800, 1-888, 1-877, or 1-866.

Directory enquiries: 411.

U.S. calls outside your area code: 1 + area code + phone number.

International calls: 011+ country code + phone number.

Operator: 0 for assistance with local calls; 00 for international calls.

Time zones

San Francisco is on Pacific Standard Time. P.S.T. is three hours behind Eastern Standard Time (New York) and eight hours behind Greenwich Mean Time (London).

Bay Area Rapid Transport

Tipping

Tipping in the U.S. is different from many other places in the world. Most wait staff and bartenders make very low wages and depend on tips for survival. If you tip badly, don't expect good service if you return.

Restaurants: 18–20 percent (even if you were dissatisfied with the service you should tip at least 10 percent). Most restaurants add a service charge automatically for parties of six or more. A quick way of working it out is to double the tax and round up or down depending on level of satisfaction.

Taxis: 10–15 percent.

Bars: 10–15 percent, or at least $1–2 per drink.

Coat check: $1–2 per coat.

Door attendants: $1–2 for hailing a cab or bringing in bags.

Porters: $1–2 per bag (more if you packed bricks).

Valet parking: $2–3.

Concierge: $5–10.

Maids: $3–5 per day.

Hairdressers and salons: 15–20 percent.

Tourist information

Visitor Information Center of San Francisco, 900 Market Street; tel: 391-2000; www.sanfrancisco.travel; Nov–Apr Mon–Fri 9am–5pm, Sat 9am–3pm (May–Oct also Sun 9am–3pm). The center is down the stairway near the cable-car turntable at Market and Pow-ell streets, and supplies brochures, maps, and helpful answers In 14 languages. You can also purchase transit passes here. Call for a listing of monthly events.

California Welcome Center, Pier 39, 2nd level, www.visitcalifornia.com.

Transportation

A major hub for flights from all over the world, San Francisco is easily reached by air, while visitors from other parts of the United States can opt to travel by rail or bus. Once here, the city and its outlying areas are comfortably navigable by public transportation.

In San Francisco, a car is not generally necessary to see the sights, and can prove to be something of a hassle, especially when such great views are provided on cable-cars from the tops of the city's hills. Efficient, affordable, and comprehensive, San Francisco's public transportation network makes it easy to be green.

Getting to San Francisco

By air

San Francisco International Airport (SFO; 1 McDonnell Road; tel: 650-821-8211; www.flysfo.com) is the major international airport for northern California. From Europe, all the major airlines offer non-stop flights or connections via New York, Chicago, or Los Angeles. It also receives non-stop, or one-stop, flights from all the principal Pacific airports. For foreign travelers,

Stopping to admire the view over the bay

many of the U.S. airlines offer deals for visiting several American cities.

Despite being 13 miles (21km) away, downtown San Francisco is easy to reach. Taxis and shuttles line the inner circle of the transportation zones of the Arrivals/Baggage Claim Level, while BART (Bay Area Rapid Transit), located at the Departures/Ticketing Level at the International Terminal and accessible from the Domestic Terminal by the Airtrain, takes passengers to downtown San Francisco and across the bay to various cities, for a minimal cost. The area is blanketed by Wi-Fi, which can be used for a fee.

The **Oakland International Airport** (OAK; 1 Airport Drive, Oakland; tel: 510-563-3300; www.flyoakland.com) is located 4 miles (6km) south of the city's downtown, and is accessible by BART (take AirBART shuttles from the Oakland Coliseum BART station to the airport for $3). A hub for low-cost carriers, OAK is often a more economical alternative to the bigger and busier SFO.

The smallest of the three airports, **Mineta San Jose International Airport** (SJC; 1732 North 1st Street, San Jose; tel: 408-501-7600; www.sjc.org) is nearly 50 miles (80km) from downtown San Francisco.

Carbon-offsetting

Every day, airplanes dump 90 million lbs (41 million kg) of carbon dioxide and other noxious greenhouse gasses into the atmosphere. To "offset" their share of the carbon footprint, travelers can buy carbon credits according to the distance traveled. Credits invest money into renewable energy and energy efficiency programs. For more information visit www.carbonfund.org.

By train

While **Amtrak** (Emeryville depot, 5885 Horton Street, Emeryville; tel: 510-450-1087 (information line: 800-872-7245; www.amtrak.com), the cross-continental passenger rail line, does not connect directly to San Francisco, it has a free shuttle to deliver passengers to and from the depot in Emeryville, located in the East Bay. For longer trips, Amtrak can be frustrating, as passenger trains share the rail lines with, and must defer to, the freight lines, causing significant delays. Nonetheless, it still remains a green alternative to air travel, and some routes are quite picturesque.

By bus

Downtown, just east of Market Street, the **Transbay Terminal** (425 Mission Street; information line: 800-231-2222; www.greyhound.com; tel: 495-1555) is a major hub for the transcontinental **Greyhound** bus service.

By car

Despite congestion, myriad hills, and the problem of what to do with your vehicle upon arriving, San Francisco is easy to reach by car. Interstates 101 and 80 pass through the city, while Interstates 5 and 99 are not too far away in the Central Valley. State Highway 1 runs along the coast of Cali-

Embarcadero trains

fornia and the western part of San Francisco.

Getting around San Francisco

For help navigating the entire Bay Area public transit system, including Muni buses and metro streetcars, and BART, call 511 or visit www.511.org and www.sfmta.org; 511 offers assistance with planning trips using public transportation, traffic, and drive time information, tips for traveling with bikes, and links to various municipal transit agencies.

BART (Bay Area Rapid Transit)

Fast, quiet, and efficient, BART (www.bart.gov) allows passengers to get around the Bay Area in comfort. All BART lines travel through San Francisco, extending to San Francisco International Airport, and under the bay to Oakland, Berkeley, and beyond. Its stations provide maps that clearly explain routes and fares, and automatic ticketing machines from which passengers can purchase their tickets. If they do not have the exact change, passengers may carry a balance on their ticket for future use, or utilize one of the change machines also located in the stations.

Four BART lines run through downtown and provide the quickest way to travel between downtown and the Mission District, or to reach Oakland and Berkeley.

Buses and metro

Muni, the San Francisco Municipal Transit Agency, runs the city's orange and white diesel and electric buses, streetcars which run on lightrail lines underground through downtown, the historic F-line streetcars (comprising a collection of vintage trams from all over the world), and of course, the cable-cars. "Muni" can be used to refer to the system as a whole and also to the metro streetcars. The Muni Owl service replaces normal service on some lines between 1–5am.

Purchasing a map is highly recommended and will make a stay in San Francisco infinitely simpler. They are available at the Muni kiosks at the Powell and Market, Hyde and Beach, and Bay and Taylor cable-car terminals, as well as the San Francisco International Airport airport information booth near baggage claim, and in some stores, such as the Walgreens at 125 Powell Street and the Alexander Book Company at 50 2nd Street. They are also posted at many Muni Metro and bus stops.

For all Muni Metro and bus lines, adult fare is $2. Exact change is necessary, but transfer slips are given, allowing you to transfer different Muni Metro or bus lines within a 90-minute timeframe. Ride without limit on Muni-operated transport, including the cable-cars, by using 1-, 3-, or 7-day visitor "Passports" (costing $15, $23, and $29, respectively). These are good on Muni buses and metro only, so BART tickets will need to be purchased separately. They are sold at the Visitor Center at Powell and Market, the infor-

Bart station in Berkeley

mation booth near baggage claim at San Francisco International Airport, major cable-car terminals, and most Walgreens and Cole Hardware stores. For a list of other places where passes can be purchased, and for route planning and general information, see www.sfmta.com. For up-to-the-minute information on when the vehicle you are waiting for will arrive, refer to www.nextmuni.com.

Cable-cars

Taking a cable-car ride is one of the classic San Francisco experiences. Cable-cars are also operated by Muni, but are the exception to most of the Muni rules. Fares can be purchased at the kiosk at each terminal, or when you board. Drivers do give exact change (it's best to have small bills) but no transfers – if you depart one vehicle, you must pay full fare to board another. They are also considerably more expensive at $6 per trip. Often crowded with tourists, they ride over San Francisco's famous hills. Waits to board at the cable-car turnaround at 5th and Market streets can be long, so locals often walk several blocks up Powell to board at another stop. Another option if you're pressed for time is to board the California line at Van Ness or the Ferry Building; the fine views on this route are of Nob Hill, Chinatown, and the Financial District.

CityPASS

CityPASS is a 7-day pass (www.citypass.com; adult $86, child $64) that includes the benefits of a Visitor Pass (unlim-ited rides on Muni, Muni Metro, and cable car rides) but also provides one admission ticket over a 9-day period to various points of interest in San Francisco, including the California Academy of Sciences, a Blue and Gold Fleet bay cruise, Exploratorium or De Young Museum, and Aquarium of the Bay or Monterey Bay Aquarium. There's also an option to substitute Alcatraz for the bay cruise.

Taxis

Taxis are a convenient but expensive way to get about when the majority of San Francisco's public transit shuts down around 12.30am. They hover around popular tourist or nightlife spots, but in out-of-the-way locations it is advisable to call a radio-dispatched taxi. Drivers prefer cash, but take credit cards as well.

DeSoto Cab Company, tel: 970-1300.
Green Cab, tel: 626-4733.
Luxor Cab Company, tel: 282-4141.
Yellow Cab, tel: 333-3333.

Cycling

Around San Francisco, there are plenty of places to ride that are reasonably flat and far from exhaust fumes. Cycling through Golden Gate Park is a favorite, especially on Sundays, when many of the roads are blocked to cars. Riding along the Golden Gate Promenade and crossing the Golden Gate Bridge is a stunning ride, although difficult if the wind is up. For maps and additional resources, refer for www.sfbike.org.

Trolley bus in Union Square

Bikes can be rented hourly or for the day, with rates varying by type of bike, but usually $20–60 per day and $7–10 per hour. Bay Area Bike Share (www.bayareabikeshare.com) is an alternative.

Bay City Bike
501 Bay Street, 2661 Taylor Street, 2828 Jones Street, and 1325 Columbus Avenue; tel: 346-2453; http://baycitybike.com; daily from 8am.

Blazing Saddles
1095 Columbus Avenue, including a number of locations on Fisherman's Wharf; tel: 202-8888; www.blazingsaddles.com; daily from 8am.

Golden Gate Bike and Skate
3038 Fulton Street; tel: 668-1117; summer: Mon–Fri 10am–6pm, Sat–Sun until 7pm, winter: Mon–Fri 10am–5pm, Sat–Sun until 6pm.

Driving
San Francisco is a difficult city to drive and park in, often taxing the most experienced local drivers. It is crisscrossed by one-way streets, and the fast-paced driving culture can easily unnerve any visitor. If it is necessary to rent a car, all the major car-rental companies have outlets at San Francisco International Airport and around the city.

Avis Rental Car
Tel: 800-230-4898; www.avis.com.

Enterprise
Tel: 800-261-7331; www.enterprise.com.

Hertz Rent A Car
Tel: 800-654-3131; www.hertz.com.

Walking
The best way to see San Francisco is by walking. Only 7 miles by 7 miles (127 sq km), it is easy to cover great distances while seeing many different neighborhoods and glimpsing how residents live. Walking the hills provides spectacular views of the city and the rest of the Bay Area. Bring a map, comfortable shoes, and an extra layer of clothing in case the infamous San Francisco fog rolls in. Always be alert while crossing intersections. Taxis can be particularly aggressive.

Getting Around the Bay Area
Caltrain
Caltrain (main San Francisco depot, 700 4th Street; information line: 800-660-4287; www.caltrain.org) runs alongside Highway 101 to San Jose, with limited extensions all the way to Gilroy. It is largely a commuter train, but for visitors headed to the Peninsula or the South Bay, it is an enjoyable ride; there's plenty of comfortable seating, an upper deck with tables, and a car to accommodate passengers with bikes. Caltrain's terminus is near the AT&T Ballpark and many San Francisco Muni bus and Metro lines, helpful for getting passengers around the city. Every Caltrain stop has an electronic ticket machine at which passengers can purchase tickets.

Ferries
Many locals use ferries for commuting, but for visitors, they can provide a great

Students at Berkeley   *Ferry to Alcatraz*

scenic and environmental alternative to driving. Departing from Fisherman's Wharf or the Ferry Building, they travel to Angel Island, and throughout the North and East Bay areas. Tickets can be purchased at the ticket windows next to the ferry terminals.

Blue and Gold Fleet, Pier 39 Marine Terminal, The Embarcadero at Beach Street; tel: 705-8200; www.blueandgold fleet.com.

Golden Gate Ferry, Ferry Building, The Embarcadero at Market Street; tel: 455-2000; www.goldengateferry.org.

Intercity buses

Neighboring transit systems also connect San Francisco with other Bay Area cities. These buses can be caught at various stops downtown, or at the Transbay Terminal, located at First and Mission streets.

Golden Gate Transit, tel: 455-2000; www.goldengate.org.

Alameda Contra-Costa County Transit District, tel: 510-891-4777; www. actransit.org.

San Mateo County Transit District tel: 1-800-660-4287; www.samtrans. com.

Visa information

U.S. citizens returning to the U.S. by air or land from Canada, Mexico, the Caribbean, and Bermuda will need a valid passport or other accepted identification. Under the current Visa Waiver Scheme, for nationals of over 30 countries (including the U.K., Australia, France, Germany, Ireland, Japan, and New Zealand) no visa is needed for stays in the U.S. of less than 90 days (for business or pleasure). However, prior to traveling, you must now obtain authorization through the Electronic System for Travel Authorization (ESTA). Go to http://cbp.gov or https://esta. cbp.dhs.gov/esta/ to apply.

All other foreign citizens need visas. Application forms and information are available at U.S. embassies and consulates (http://usvisas.state.gov). Plan several weeks or more in advance as, depending on your country of residence and the time you wish to travel, the process can take a while. Be sure to double-check current requirements at http://travel.state.gov.

Weights and measures

The U.S. uses the imperial system.

A tribute to Jack Kerouac

BOOKS AND FILM

San Francisco has a remarkably rich literary tradition, with writers as varied as Mark Twain, Dashiell Hammett, Armistead Maupin, and Amy Tan drawing inspiration from the city's characters, subcultures, and cityscapes. The city was also ground zero for the Beat movement in the 1950s, galvanized by writers such as Jack Kerouac and Allen Ginsberg. Today, bibliophiles peruse independent bookstores like City Lights, join writers groups, attend author readings, and go on a literary binge each fall during the Litquake festival.

San Francisco is also no stranger to the silver screen. Its iconic views have played supporting roles in movies from *Vertigo* to *Dirty Harry* to *Basic Instinct*. The city hosts several first-rate film festivals each year, and everyday options include 3D offerings at the Metreon, rare-single screen and art house theaters, and 21-plus viewing at the Kabuki.

Books

Non-fiction
You Can't Win by Jack Black. A favorite of Beat writers, Black's autobiography details his life of crime in San Francisco at the turn of the 20th century.
The Best of Herb Caen by Herb Caen, A collection of the quintessential chronicler of San Francisco culture from 1960–75.
Stairway Walks of San Francisco by Adah Bakalinsky. A delightful new edition of Bakalinsky's guide to 27 urban hikes up and down some of the city's 350 stairways.
Above San Francisco by Robert Cameron and Arthur Hoppe. A gorgeous book of aerial photography of the City by the Bay. Perfect as either a preview of your visit, a memento of it, or a gift to entice a friend.

Fiction
The Maltese Falcon by Dashiell Hammett. A noir classic that tells the tale of Sam Spade, a hardboiled San Francisco detective, hired to solve the mystery of a missing gold statuette for which he must dodge villains and beautiful women alike.
Tales of the City by Armistead Maupin. Originally a serial in the *San Francisco Chronicle*, Maupin's novel stitches together the lives of residents of the fictitious Barbary Lane told with delightful candor.
On the Road by Jack Kerouac. In what became the bible of the Beat generation, the iconoclastic writer chronicles his jazz and drug-fueled travels and travails crisscrossing the United States and Mexico in the 1950s.
The Joy Luck Club by Amy Tan. The award-winning first novel of local lit darling Amy Tan, chronicling the lives of daughters of Chinese immigrants in San Francisco and the challenges of being

City Lights Bookstore   *Humphrey Bogart in the Maltese Falcon*

modern American women with old-world parents.

Memoir
Oh the Glory of it All by Sean Wilsey. This amusing and poignant memoir by the son of wealthy San Francisco socialites was met with controversy due to Wilsey's revelations about his extended family.

History
The Great Earthquake and Firestorms 1906 by Philip L. Fradkin. An amazingly compelling and insightful account of the destruction, corruption, and fortitude that defined the city in 1906.

Imperial San Francisco by Gray Brechin. Brechin offers an alternative history of San Francisco through its myriad statues and monuments, and one in which the city is a global power player.

The Electric Kool-Aid Acid Test by Tom Wolfe. A classic of "New Journalism" finds the author immersed in the psychedelic adventures of Ken Kesey and his band of Merry Pranksters as they "turn on" first San Francisco, then America, with LSD.

Gimme Something Better: The Profound, Progressive, and Occasionally Pointless History of Bay Area Punk from Dead Kennedys to Green Day by Jack Boulware and Silke Tudor. An oral history of the Bay Area punk scene from the '70s into the '00s, warts and all.

The Mayor of Castro Street: The Life and Times of Harvey Milk by Randy Shilts. Perhaps the quintessential biography of the first openly gay man elected to office in America.

Films

Barbary Coast, 1935. A dramatic love story set in the city's wild Gold Rush days, and directed by Howard Hawks.

San Francisco, 1936. Clark Gable stars as a Barbary saloon keeper competing for the affections of a beautiful singer. Director W.S. Van Dyke spectacularly recreates the 1906 earthquake.

The Maltese Falcon, 1941. Humphrey Bogart skulks Nob Hill backways as detective Sam Spade.

Vertigo, 1958. A retired San Francisco detective (James Stewart) investigates the mysterious activities of old friend's wife (Kim Novak) in this Hitchcock classic.

Bullitt, 1968. Steve McQueen bounces a Mustang over San Francisco's hills as a cop trying to protect a witness, while piecing together what's really going on.

Dirty Harry, 1971. Saints Peter and Paul Church hosts a shootout in this crime thriller starring Clint Eastwood as a police inspector trying to track down a psychopath.

The Wild Parrots of Telegraph Hill, 2003. A touching documentary about the city's flocks of red-headed wild parrots, and the man who knows them best.

Milk, 2008. Sean Penn stars as Harvey Milk, American gay activist and California's first openly gay elected official.

Blue Jasmine, 2013. A broke Manhattan socialite (Cate Blanchett) imposes on her estranged sister in San Francisco.

ABOUT THIS BOOK

This *Explore Guide* has been produced by the editors of Insight Guides, whose books have set the standard for visual travel guides since 1970. With top-quality photography and authoritative recommendations, these guidebooks bring you the very best routes and itineraries in the world's most exciting destinations.

BEST ROUTES

The routes in the book provide something to suit all budgets, tastes and trip lengths. As well as covering the destination's many classic attractions, the itineraries track lesser-known sights, and there are also excursions for those who want to extend their visit outside the city. The routes embrace a range of interests, so whether you are an art fan, a gourmet, a history buff or have kids to entertain, you will find an option to suit.

We recommend reading the whole of a route before setting out. This should help you to familiarise yourself with it and enable you to plan where to stop for refreshments – options are shown in the 'Food and Drink' box at the end of each tour.

For our pick of the tours by theme, consult Recommended Routes for... (see pages 4–5).

INTRODUCTION

The routes are set in context by this introductory section, giving an overview of the destination to set the scene, plus background information on food and drink, shopping and more, while a succinct history timeline highlights the key events over the centuries.

DIRECTORY

Also supporting the routes is a Directory chapter, with a clearly organised A–Z of practical information, our pick of where to stay while you are there and select restaurant listings; these eateries complement the more low-key cafés and restaurants that feature within the routes and are intended to offer a wider choice for evening dining. Also included here are some nightlife listings and our recommendations for books and films about the destination.

ABOUT THE AUTHORS

Barbara Rockwell is a freelance arts and travel writer and devoted city-lover. Born and raised in the San Francisco Bay Area, she studied at the University of California at Berkeley before settling in San Francisco. Her U.S. travel expertise runs from coast to coast. She has written for various travel and lifestyle websites and contributed to several travel guides, including *Insight Guide California*.

Some of the tours in this guide were originally conceived by Berkeley-based writer Anne Cherian.

CONTACT THE EDITORS

We hope you find this Explore Guide useful, interesting and a pleasure to read. If you have any questions or feedback on the text, pictures or maps, please do let us know. If you have noticed any errors or outdated facts, or have suggestions for places to include on the routes, we would be delighted to hear from you. Please drop us an email at insight@apaguide.co.uk. Thanks!

CREDITS

Explore San Francisco
Contributors: Barbara Rockwell
Commissioning Editor: Rachel Lawrence
Series Editor: Sarah Clark
Pictures/Art: Tom Smyth/Shahid Mahmood
Map Production: original cartography
Berndtson & Berndtson, updated by Apa
Cartography Department
Production: Tynan Dean and Rebeka Davies
Photo credits: Alamy 18, 68/69, 85R, 91,
137R; Bigstock 13R, 21, 106; Dreamstime
1, 4TR, 6/7T, 10, 62, 76/77, 87, 88, 90,
92, 92/93, 114/115, 116/117, 124, 125;
Getty Images 136; iStockphoto 4/5M, 5MR,
20, 26/27T, 32, 33, 34/35, 40, 42, 47, 53,
76; Kobal 22, 23; Nowitz Photography/Apa
Publications 2ML, 2MC, 2MR, 2MR, 2MC,
2ML, 2/3T, 4MC, 4ML, 4BC, 4/5T, 5MR, 6ML,
6MC, 6ML, 6MC, 6MR, 6MR, 8, 9R, 8/9, 11R,
10/11, 12, 12/13, 14, 14/15, 16, 16/17,
17R, 18/19, 19R, 24/25, 26ML, 26MC,
26MR, 26ML, 26MC, 26MR, 28, 28/29, 29R,
30, 30/31, 31R, 34, 35R, 36, 36/37, 37R,
38, 38/39, 39R, 40/41, 42/43, 43R, 44,
45R, 44/45, 46, 48, 49R, 48/49, 50, 50/51,
51R, 52, 54, 54/55, 55R, 56, 56/57, 57R,
58, 59R, 58/59, 60, 61R, 60/61, 62/63,
64, 64/65, 65R, 66, 66/67, 67R, 68T, 68B,
69R, 70, 70/71, 71R, 72, 72/73, 74, 74/75,
75R, 77R, 78, 78/79, 80, 81R, 80/81, 82,
82/83, 83R, 84, 84/85, 86, 88/89, 93R,
94ML, 94MC, 94MR, 94MR, 94MC, 94ML,
94/95T, 96, 96/97, 97R, 98, 98/99, 100,
100/101, 101R, 102, 102/103, 103R,
104, 104/105, 105R, 106/107, 107R, 108,
108/109, 109R, 110, 110/111, 111R, 112,
112/113, 113R, 114, 115R, 116, 117R,
118, 118/119, 119R, 120, 120/121, 122,
122/123, 123R, 126, 126/127, 128, 129R,
128/129, 130, 130/131, 132, 132/133,
134, 135R, 134/135, 136/137; TopFoto 24
Cover credits: Main: The Painted Ladies
Victorian houses, *4Corners Images*; Front
Cover BL: Golden Gate Bridge, *Daniella
Nowitz/Apa Publications*; Back Cover: (Left)
Lombard Street, *Dreamstime*; (Right): Cable
car Tram, *iStockphoto*

Printed by CTPS – China

© 2014 Apa Publications (UK) Ltd
All Rights Reserved

First Edition 2014

DISTRIBUTION

Worldwide
APA Publications GmbH & Co. Verlag KG
(Singapore branch)
7030 Ang Mo Kio Ave 5, 08-65
Northstar @ AMK, Singapore 569880
Email: apasin@singnet.com.sg
UK and Ireland
Dorling Kindersley Ltd (a Penguin Company)
80 Strand, London, WC2R 0RL, UK
Email: sales@uk.dk.com
US
Ingram Publisher Services
One Ingram Blvd, PO Box 3006, La Vergne,
TN 37086-1986
Email: ips@ingramcontent.com
Australia and New Zealand
Woodslane
10 Apollo St, Warriewood NSW 2102,
Australia
Email: info@woodslane.com.au

INDEX

MAP LEGEND

● Start of tour

→ Tour & route direction

❶ Recommended sight

❷ Recommended restaurant/café

★ Place of interest

ℹ Tourist information

𝟙 Statue/monument

✉ Main post office

🚌 Main bus station

Ⓜ Muni station

Park

Important building

Hotel

Transport hub

Mall/market/store

Pedestrian area

- - - Streetcar line